WATER UNDER THE KEEL

memoirs of a seagoing life

CAPTAIN
GEORGE GRIMES

Published by Milk Island Press
2 Francis Way, Rockport, Massachusetts 01966
bocean@comcast.net

Designed by Maine Authors Publishing, Rockland, Maine
www.maineauthorspublishing.com

Printed in the United States of America

To Sally, Kirsten, and Katelyn, the loves of my life.
To Gretel and Sydney, my animal friends.

≋ ACKNOWLEDGMENTS ≋

I could not have completed this project without the love and encouragement of my wife, Sally and two wonderful and caring daughters, Kirsten and Katelyn. Sally, you have kept me on course through rough seas and were always there for me.

I am indebted to my mother and father, who allowed me to feel free to spend so many hours on and around the water during my childhood and adolescent years. My siblings, Barbara, Shirley, and John, were always there with love and support as I pursued my professional ambitions. Many thanks also to my teachers at Rockport High School. Without their guidance and advice, I would not have been provided with the necessary tools, with which to enter college.

A hearty "well done" to the leaders of the Rockport Sea Explorers, George "Ned" Cameron, Gene "Shorty" Lesch, Dr. J. Wain Baker, Chief Richard Hale, Robert Ahonen, George Caffrey, and many other volunteers who gave countless hours, providing guidance at a time when it was so essential. The instructors at Maine Maritime Academy shared their knowledge and experience as I perfected my professional skills for a career on the sea. Captain Greg Sevarino took the initiative to allow me to perfect my skills in the wheelhouse of a tugboat. For that I am very grateful.

Paul Woodbury, Hilary Smart, and Jack Goddard taught me the skills needed to race Star-class sailboats. "Duffy" Blatchford taught me much about practical seamanship. Thanks also to Arthur

Swanson and his unique way of disciplining mischievous kids at the yacht club. Carl Magee was there at a time when I was fragile and needed support. I will always value his friendship and advice as we worked together at Manchester Yacht Club. To the sailing instructors at Sandy Bay Yacht Club, who were brave enough to teach us sailing lessons on O Boats, you too deserve thanks for a job well done, given the challenges that we kids presented from day to day. I will always remember the good times, sailing Turnabouts and spending hours sitting with my friends by the warm fire in the yacht club meeting room on those cold fall days. Those years at the club were very special and hold many great memories. To my very good friend, Tim Baker, who left us at such a young age, may you have Peace!

Thanks to Peggy McCardle, who spent valuable time editing these words. I appreciate your encouragement through the times when I doubted whether this book would ever come to be.

CONTENTS

PROLOGUE

A routine cargo watch begins on board in the port of Kobe, Japan. All cargo hatches and decks are open, being discharged by longshoremen. Lashing and carpenter gangs are busy securing cargo in preparation for the upcoming voyage. But the normal routine is interrupted by a telephone call from Port Authority personnel. "You must sail the ship immediately! There is imminent danger of a typhoon approaching. The pilot will come to your vessel very soon." Incredibly, our habitually self-righteous master makes it clear that the ship will not be moved! An hour passes, and the port officials call with another warning for the vessel to sail at once. Despite having been informed once again, the master still refuses to move the vessel.

An hour later, headlight beams shine across the dock and it is obvious that the pilot is coming toward the vessel. Simultaneously, two tugboats are observed approaching the ship. Reaching the head of the gangway, the pilot emphasizes the urgent necessity for the vessel to sail quickly. The master, belatedly realizing the immediate threat posed by the typhoon (the Pacific Ocean term for a hurricane), gives commands such as "Call the chief. Start the engines. Test the gear. Close the hatches." When asked whether to replace the hatch boards on the tweendecks (intermediate decks between the main deck and lower hold), he replies, "Put only the beams on." All wooden shoring had been previously removed from the cargo of tea stowed on these decks, in order to allow access to the lower holds. It was essential that the small wooden hatch boards be placed between the beams, in order to prevent the flimsy crates of tea from cascading into the lower hold.

Soon the steel beams are put in place and the main deck hatches are secured for sea. All navigation gear has been tested, and the two tugs have been made fast alongside. The ship is gently eased away from the pier and turned, and then the tugs move away. Most of the piers are vacant by this time, giving the appearance of a deserted port. As the vessel passes the breakwaters protecting the inner harbor, the full fury of the typhoon becomes apparent to all on board.

Because of the delay in sailing, the ship is compelled to navigate a limited area, with other vessels anchored in close proximity. The captain has decided not to anchor because of earlier problems affecting the efficiency of the anchor windlass. Visibility has dropped to a few hundred yards, the wind is reaching gusts of over one hundred miles per hour, and the seas are building rapidly.

An anchored ship is sighted dead ahead and reported to the captain, who screams in response, "Hard left, full astern." Several similar incidents add to the deteriorating situation. The shriek of wind in the rigging, caused by gusts reaching one hundred twenty miles per hour, is deafening and remains imprinted in my mind to this day. The deckhand sustains a blow to his head from a fall and is discovered lying unconscious next to the running light casing on the starboard bridge wing. The steward yells to the captain that there will be no meals today because of the excessive rolling of the ship. The captain orders the steward from the bridge, contributing to the general stress. Because the vessel is not at anchor, she is rolling violently in the rapidly building waves.

Eventually the wind velocity decreases and the seas grow calmer, allowing the vessel to return safely to port. The hatches are opened in order to assess the damage to ship and cargo. Upon inspection, large piles of tea are observed in the lower holds. The damaged cargo must be removed and the paperwork completed for the insurance claims that will surely follow. The deckhand has received permanent brain injuries and lost sight in one eye as a result of his fall in the height of the storm. He will never return to work.

The events of that day are still vivid in my memory. The chaos on board may have been instigated by a typhoon, but the underlying cause was the poor leadership qualities of our vessel's master in times of stress. His inability to recognize the urgency of a situation and respect the advice of others, as well as his apparent lack of self-confidence when the chips were down, gave his crew an uneasy feeling. I have never forgotten what it was like to be with a captain whose performance could not be depended upon in a time of extreme stress and danger.

This description emphasizes the importance of the master exercising good judgment regarding shipboard operations. Although the first year of my career included this harrowing experience, there were many pleasurable and rewarding times. This memoir is intended to give the reader an opportunity to share some of my experiences, both good and bad, as well as to become exposed to life at sea.

INTRODUCTION

In 1965, the United States was socially and politically in turmoil. Overseas, the war in Vietnam was escalating, making the rapid shipment of arms and materiel essential. President John F. Kennedy had been brutally assassinated two years before. At home, racial tensions were increasing following the senseless killing of Dr. Martin Luther King. Segregation was part of every day life for black students, who were being excluded from attending school with white students. During my teen and post-teen years, I began to question whether the very fabric of our Union was being tested once again, as it had been before in our history.

The military draft was in force during the Sixties, requiring young males to gamble their futures and possibly their lives on the luck of the draw. Many citizens were questioning the wisdom of defending the people of an unknown nation on a far-away continent in what looked from the outside a lot like a civil war. A deferment could be obtained if one was fortunate enough to attend a college, thereby avoiding the draft. Another alternative was to give up United States citizenship and become a citizen of another country, often Canada. Although many chose that option, it was not for me, because of my love for my country. I made the decision to attend Maine Maritime Academy because it would prepare me for a future career at sea and enable me to serve my country in a more pacifist way.

America was in a time of transition, commercially and domestically. Vacationers no longer made long passages across the seas, living on board the luxury steamships of the time. The introduction of fast and efficient air travel had reduced the transit time across oceans from days to hours. Transportation of goods by rail was rapidly giving way to the trucking industry following the construction of our interstate highway system—an initiative begun in the Fifties by President Eisenhower. Steam propulsion of the tugs and ferries working in our ports was transitioning to diesel power. Ships using the break-bulk cargo-carrying method were giving way to the much more efficient containerships of the intermodal age. This system used standardized containers twenty and forty feet in length, thereby minimizing damage, pilferage, and cargo-transfer time and labor.

I entered this evolving maritime industry upon graduation from Maine Maritime Academy in June of 1965. The port of New York was a busy place at that time. Steam tugs could be observed hustling railroad cars on board specially designed barges, while ferries darted across the main shipping traffic routes. Smaller, more specialized vessels scurried about in the performance of their duties. The shrill sound of steam whistles could be heard throughout the day and night. Several large steam luxury ocean liners could be seen at their respective berths along the "North River" (the Hudson) at any given time. Break-bulk cargo vessels could be observed loading or discharging general cargo into specialized barges while at anchor or moored alongside piers. It was there that I began my seagoing career, unaware of the adventures that lay ahead. My life at sea has involved many course changes and challenges along the way, but it has been a rewarding and exciting one.

I invite the reader to come on board with me as I navigate those waters once again. The seas were frequently rough and challenging, but they were often calm and peaceful as well. Anyone who has followed the sea will long remember the beautiful sunsets and sunrises and the minutes before sunset, searching for the ever-elusive "green flash." This condition occurs shortly after sunset or before sunrise, when a green spot is visible for no more than a few seconds above the sun, or when a green ray shoots up from the sunset point. The mariner is in an ideal position to observe this event due to the unobstructed horizon at sea. I cannot recall ever having observed the actual flash, though at times I perceived a slight greenish tint. I'm still looking.

There were gales, heavy seas, and times when our very existence depended upon the ship holding together. Near collisions, equipment breakdowns, and typhoons all figure in these pages. The nature of the seagoing occupation, and how it affects family life, will be covered as we proceed along our course. I am convinced that I was predestined to go to sea by those in my bloodline who preceded me, so we begin the voyage with an introduction to my ancestral roots. From there, the reader will follow me through my early years, observing along the route some of the factors that led me to a life at sea. As the command is given to "let go fore and aft," I invite you, dear reader, to join me on a voyage of adventure and discovery.

PART ONE
THE FORMATIVE YEARS

FAMILY HISTORY

There have been four master mariners, including myself, in the most recent six generations on my father's side of the family. Captain Joseph Stickney, who was born in Boxford, Massachusetts, on October 5, 1767, and died on March 23, 1817, was a Master Mariner in the employ of the Honorable Israel Thorndike of Beverly, Massachusetts, as early as 1809. His son, Captain John Stickney, was born in Beverly on March 9, 1799, and died as a Master Mariner on board the brig *Planet* of Salem. His body rests in peace on the island of Rio Nunez off the Northwest African Coast.

Captain John Edward Stickney, son of Captain John Stickney, was born on January 26, 1839, in Beverly and died on May 24, 1912. He served with distinction during the Civil War on board Lehigh Class gunboats, which were similar in construction to the famous ironclad *Monitor*. He delivered several British prizes to Key West, Florida—ships captured by the Union Navy in its blockade of Southern ports. His remains are interred on the Stickney family plot in Beverly along with those of his daughter Grace, my father's mother, and her husband George Bragdon Grimes, whose first name I was given at baptism.

The succession of master mariners skipped one generation with my father. He did not follow a seagoing career, but still loved the sea. The seafaring lineage was not limited to my father's side of the family. My mother's father, Dana Gott, followed a career connected with the sea for thirty-six years, first in the United States

Lifesaving Service and later in the United States Coast Guard.

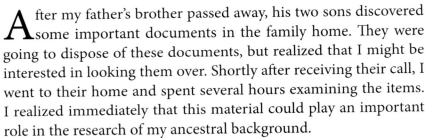

A VERY OLD NAVIGATION CHART

After my father's brother passed away, his two sons discovered some important documents in the family home. They were going to dispose of these documents, but realized that I might be interested in looking them over. Shortly after receiving their call, I went to their home and spent several hours examining the items. I realized immediately that this material could play an important role in the research of my ancestral background.

In addition, one of the sons offered to give me the sea chest that Grandfather Stickney carried with him on board his vessels. I told him that I would pick it up when I returned from my next tour of duty at sea. This turned out to be a grave error, because the other son sold the chest to an antique dealer while I was away. Even though the loss of the sea chest was disappointing, I was happy to have acquired the documents.

The most important of these documents is a navigation chart that was published in 1838. The chart is now mounted in a mahogany frame and occupies a special place in my office, where viewers can appreciate its historical significance. Upon contacting a local maritime museum, I learned that the process of gluing charts to heavy blue construction paper and hand sewing the edges using sail twine was a common practice at the time. It was clear that several component charts had been cut and pieced together in order to show the waters of the South Pacific from Cape Horn to the Far East, including the mid-Pacific islands. My research convinced me that I was holding the very chart that my great, great grandfather had used to guide his vessels over the waters of the South Pacific Ocean approximately one hundred and seventy years earlier.

Close inspection of the chart reveals penciled drawings of whales' tails, reefs, and other notations, intended to indicate objects discovered or witnessed during his voyages. The names of several vessels, as well as the noon positions of these vessels, are marked on the chart and give a clear indication of the routes navigated. Captain John Stickney carried this chart—as well as his sextant, navigation publications, and other personal possessions—in his wooden sea chest, which he later passed on to his son Captain John E. Stickney. I am proud to have followed in the wake of these very capable master mariners in this honorable profession.

A number of letters written by Great Grandfather Stickney have been well preserved through the years and remain in my possession today. The following letter written to his wife, Martha, on November 1, 1830, gives the reader an insight into the challenges that a master mariner faced on board sailing vessels during the mid-nineteenth century.

At Sea   *November 1, 1830*

    Dear Martha,

    It is with pleasure to inform you that I am now safe around Cape Horn in the Latitude of 28 degrees South, Longitude 84 degrees West, in the southeast trades, running with a gentle breeze toward the North and westward. I suppose you would like to know something about my passage, after leaving Boston and the pilot.

    The wind sprung out from the Northeast, which obliged me to brace sharp, in order to clear Cape Cod. The breeze increasing and growing thick and raining at 2 AM, I was obliged to tack ship and stand to the Northwest. When daylight came, I tacked and stood out the South Channel.

    The wind, stiff from the East and blowing hard, obliged us to shorten sail. After experiencing seven days hard wind and losing our stern boat, we, at last, took the wind from the Northwest, blowing a stiff gale. The vessel going ten miles per hour and a high sea tumbling after us, and after twenty days, we fell in with the ship, Hercules, Captain Rand. He out sailed us, but not for long, for we saw her three days later in company with the ship Bombay, a fine new ship.

    After getting across the line, I had windy, fine weather until arriving at 45 degrees South Latitude, then gales from the Southeast to West Southwest, which tossed me for fifteen days. Nothing on, but storm sails and head winds. Just my luck, after getting to the westward of Cape Horn, we ran into very bad weather, on the first of October, blowing a heavy gale, no sail set, but close reefed topsail and main storm sails. A man at the wheel got knocked down and broke his arm and bruised his side. At length, we got a fair wind on Saturday, October 29, and made the island of Maspuno, of Valparaiso.

UNITED STATES LIFESAVING SERVICE

Founded by the federal government in 1848, the United States Lifesaving Service was an organization dedicated to saving the lives of crewmembers on board vessels in distress. An organization called the Humane Society of Massachusetts, having similar objectives, was formed during the same year. As years passed the two organizations merged and expanded from Cape Cod and Block Island to Maine in the northeast and the Outer Banks of North Carolina in the south. Lifesaving stations were built along the coastline approximately twenty miles apart. If a surfman on beach patrol sighted a vessel foundering on a lee shore, he ignited a signal flare, thereby alerting station personnel, who responded either by pulling a wagon or using a team of horses to launch a seaworthy surfboat from the beach. The surfboat crew numbered from four to eight oarsmen and a coxswain, who was responsible for steering the boat. Many lives were saved by the expert seamanship of men using this method.

The breeches buoy was another effective means of saving lives of those in distress. This device consisted of a line-throwing apparatus in combination with heavier lines, blocks, and a life ring. Canvas trousers extended below the life ring, allowing an individual to step into them. The person being rescued then clung to the supporting lines, with the ring at his waist, while the lifesaving crew on shore pulled him to safety. The ride through the surf was wild, but there were helping hands at the other end. All the equipment required for this operation was carried on a cart

pulled by several surfmen or a team of horses to the vicinity of the vessel in distress.

My grandfather Dana Gott—my mother's father—was born on the shores of Pigeon Cove on Cape Ann, Massachusetts, the home of his ancestors. In the year 1908, as a young man, Dana enlisted in the lifesaving service and was stationed at the Gurnet Life Saving Station in Plymouth, Massachusetts. He then served at several local stations, his longest term being served at Straitsmouth Lifesaving Station at Gap Head, in Rockport, Massachusetts, where he served as a surfman for fourteen years. His service spanned thirty years all told, first in the United States Lifesaving Service and later in the United States Coast Guard.

As Dana became interested in aviation, he transferred to a United States Coast Guard aviation station, known as Base Seven, on Ten Pound Island in Gloucester Harbor. There he was put in charge of constructing the hangar and recreation hall. His main duty was to ensure the readiness of base aircraft. Base Seven had been organized in 1925 for the purpose of maintaining surveillance on rumrunners during prohibition. Dana was transferred to several air stations in Charleston, South Carolina, and Miami, Florida, for the remainder of his service. He was considered a pioneer of the U.S. Coast Guard Air Patrol and retired holding the rank of Chief Aviation Motor Machinist's Mate.

DANA'S LIFE FOLLOWING RETIREMENT

Below are excerpts from a newspaper article, written when Dana retired from the United States Coast Guard:

> *In those days we really had to put out. There were no motors in our surfboats. Getting alongside of vessels that needed help was a matter of strong men, each taking an eighteen-foot ash oar and pulling. I remember many a time going to the rescue in mid-winter, in a fifty mile an hour gale. Getting the boat out through the surf was the toughest part of the job. Lots of times the boat would turn over and be pounded back onto the beach two or three times, leaving us floundering around in that icy water, before we'd finally get it past the breakers.*
>
> *That was plenty tough, but the rowing was just plain work. It was about the hardest in the world. In the gusts we'd row hard and just about hold our own or even lose a few feet, and then in the lulls we'd pull our hardest and make a few yards toward our goal. In those days we'd row until we couldn't row another stroke and then row for hours more.*

Dana remembered being at the oars for six and seven hours off the New England coast, rowing into the teeth of winter gales and seeing as many as thirteen vessels in distress at the same time.

On his routine foot patrol, Dana would set out wearing hip boots and carrying a signal flare, lantern, and other necessary pieces of gear. He would walk along the shore, ever vigilant to sight vessels in distress offshore. If he sighted a stranded vessel, he would ignite a flare as described above, alerting his station mates that a vessel had been sighted and assistance was needed. As Dana would begin his patrol, another surfman from a nearby station would begin a patrol from the opposite direction, and the two would meet, exchange tokens as proof of their meeting, and resume their patrols. My mother often walked on these foot patrols with Dana when she was a little girl.

My mother and I walked to Pigeon Cove on Sunday afternoons when I was a child to visit my Grandmother Elizabeth, Aunt Dorothy, and Grandfather Dana. Pigeon Cove, known locally as "the North Village," is located on the northeast extremity of Cape Ann. Their house was near the Cape Ann Tool Company, across the street from the post office. I always enjoyed the view from their front room of the fishing boats moored in the picturesque harbor.

During those visits we sat at the round oak table in the

middle of the living room and listened to Dana reminisce about his lifesaving days. I would look on with fascination as Dana carefully deposited a small amount of tobacco on a small sheet of cigarette paper. After shaping the tobacco carefully into the form of a cigarette, he licked the edge of the paper and bound the tobacco tightly. Dana was a tall, strong, handsome man who always wore a heavy flannel shirt in the winter months. He and I would often walk to his hideaway in the backyard, where he went to spend time alone and to relax and reflect on past experiences. There, adorning the walls, were pinups of Marilyn Monroe and old picture postcards of places to which he had traveled or been stationed during his years of service. Dana presented himself in a strong and dignified manner. His face was wrinkled and weather-beaten, a testimony to his life spent around the water and his years of service in the elements. I looked up to my grandfather and admired the way he stood tall and walked proudly. Although he appeared tough on the surface, he was a gentle and caring man beneath the skin, a role model in so many ways. I am saddened that I was so young when he passed on and feel short-changed by the limited time I had with him.

When I was young, there were several small businesses in the downtown area of Pigeon Cove. The post office, the fire station, and the remains of the Cape Ann Tool Company remain standing today. I used to watch the factory workers standing in front of the blazing furnaces with long steel tongs holding red-hot pieces of metal. That scene was scary to me at the time because of the shadows and flames in the darkness accompanied by the loud banging of the hammers. Many of the workers sustained serious injuries while operating the heavy equipment, or lost their hearing from the constant noise. The sound of the hammers served as a navigational aid when we kids became disoriented in the fog while sailing our turnabouts.

LAUNCHING

I was born on November 10, 1943, in the small New England fishing town of Rockport, Massachusetts. At that time it was common for births to occur at home under the ministrations of a midwife or family doctor. My father often said that the reason I followed a life at sea was that I came into the world with two half hitches of umbilical cord around my neck. A competent midwife saved, what could have been a disastrous outcome, and my mother delivered a healthy son.

I was the youngest of four children born to Marion Evelyn Gott and John Haskins Grimes. Barbara was the oldest of my siblings, and Shirley arrived about four years later. John Dana Grimes, my only brother, came four years after Shirley, and I, little Georgie, arrived four years after John. My mother insisted on referring to me as the baby of the family, which bothered me early in life. When I was a baby, my family moved to a small Cape Cod style house at 54 High Street. (This house still stands just downhill from number 58, where my wife, Sally, and I lived after we were married.) A few years later, the family moved to a large house at 69 Main Street. One end fronted on Main Street and the other faced the Atlantic Ocean and Front Beach. The living room, over my uncle's insurance office, allowed us to look out onto Main Street and watch the activity on the street. There was a small TV set in the living room, from which we received three channels in black and white. I recall looking forward each week to a half-hour program called "Victory at Sea." Even then I was drawn to subjects dealing with life at sea. My dad's favorite chair was beside the front window. A small coal stove in the opposite corner of the room gave off plenty of heat on cold New England winter nights.

Shirley and Barbara recall babysitting me during my very early years, when I began drinking water at the public drinking fountain at Front Beach with no clothes on. For many years after, they reminded me of how embarrassed they were when friends passed and laughed. At that time my head was covered with tiny ringlets of hair. My sisters were so embarrassed when people asked how old that little girl was that they urged my mom to cut my hair. She finally gave in, and what a difference it made! I still have a piece of that curly hair in my baby book.

Living so close to the ocean had many benefits, but I have strong memories of the drafts of cold air coming through the seams around the bedroom windows during those cold New England nights. I would lay my pajamas over the living room stove to warm them before going to bed. Because there was no central heating in that house, we went to bed with several heavy blankets over us to keep warm. Walking from the living room to the back of the house, you first passed through Shirley's bedroom to get to a large bedroom where my brother John and I shared bunk beds. My parents slept in another bed on the opposite side of the room with a divider giving us some privacy. Leaving the large bedroom, you would enter Barbara's bedroom. There was an unused room at the very back of the house, facing the open ocean. It was left vacant, I suppose, because of the drafts and dangerous surf flung at the house by winter nor'easters. My dad kept his firemen's clothes immediately beside his bed, so that if the alarm rang in, he could dress for action on short notice.

Breakfast usually consisted of bacon sandwiches and delicious, crusty doughnuts from a coffee shop, located a few doors from our home. The name and ownership of this coffee shop has changed over the years, but the doughnuts still taste exactly the same. Today, visitors to Rockport can sample these doughnuts at the Brother's Brew Coffee Shop in the very same building. These doughnuts could have been the beginning of my lifelong battle with high cholesterol, but it doesn't stop me from going there often.

The Tarr School had originally housed the machine shop and offices for the Annisquam Mill, which occupied the entire block on Broadway from School Street to Dock Square. Although the factory part of the mill had been destroyed in a serious fire in 1882, this building, constructed of gray Rockport granite, survived the conflagration. It was converted into a classroom building in 1904 and named the George J. Tarr School. Many years later, during the mid-1990s, it was converted once again into what is now the Rockport Public Library, thanks to a sizable donation from a wealthy Rockport couple.

Overcrowding in the elementary school made it necessary to situate extra classrooms in other locations, so I attended kindergarten at the Legion Hall at Back Beach. I will never forget those cold midwinter mornings with the wind howling out of the northeast as I trudged to school. I attended the George J. Tarr School on School Street from grades one through six, walking every day along Main Street, turning right at the Congregational Church onto School Street, and within minutes, arriving at school. I remember walking past a towering statue of Abraham Lincoln, which stood in the middle of the hallway on the ground floor. I was always in awe of the expression on his face. (Abe now stands in the entrance hall of the elementary school on Jerdens Lane.)

My association with the sea began when I was in early boyhood. As noted, our home was situated along the seawall bordering Front Beach. Our backyard terminated in a small opening facing the Atlantic Ocean, through which a path from the yard led to a small area surrounded by a picket fence mounted atop a granite wall. I often stood on that wall, holding on to those wooden pickets and looking out to sea. A gate allowed access to a square wooden platform, from which a flight of stairs descended to a concrete pad in the sand just above the high water mark. I could simply open the gate, step on the platform, and descend those stairs to the sand below—all part of my "backyard."

Our house was so close to that granite wall that I could feel my bed shake at night when strong winter gales buffeted the house. I often lay there during those nights, imagining life on board ships

and fishing boats at sea. The beach was a world where a child could explore and learn new things daily. The undertow caused by winter storms drew much of the sand away from the beach, often exposing rocks not visible during the summer. My friends and I gave many of these rocks specific names according to their shapes and sizes. I have passed on these names to my daughters Kirsten and Katelyn, and trust that they will do the same if they have children. They still enjoy hearing stories of my days as a child on the beach. The rocks remain, weathered by years of exposure to wind and waves, although they don't seem as large and overpowering as I remember them from my youth. I occasionally walk that beach with Sydney, our golden retriever, and remember climbing, sunbathing, or swimming to Black Rocks, Flat Rock, Split Rock, and Horse Rock, just to name a few.

Little Beach was a small area of sand on the eastern side of Front Beach, bordered by the granite wall of White Wharf on one side and a large, flat, sloping granite ledge on the other. My friends and I were often tempted to go there, but were afraid of several older kids who considered it their territory. They seemed threatening to us, so we stayed away most of the time. The beach became territorial to us in those days, with certain groups staying in specific areas. The kids of Little Beach were bullies who looked for trouble a good deal of the time. I suppose we had gangs, but without the violence, drugs, and crime of today. The town held swimming classes on the beach every summer, and all kids were welcome, but because of the "bullies" I was timid to join. I learned to swim by staying within earshot of the teacher and mimicking the actions of those in the class. It was sufficient for me to acquire the necessary survival skills, but I did miss out on a lot of fun with friends.

The biggest challenge when I was ten to twelve years old was to swim out to the raft at high tide, dive off, and swim back. The raft seemed so far away then. Many of my friends were bigger than I, and it seemed so easy for them. I suppose that my self-confidence was not yet where it should have been then. As the years progressed, however, I grew stronger and more confident in my abilities, and by the time I reached high school I was swimming out there every day and thinking nothing of it.

The foundation wall of the barn in our backyard was often

severely eroded by storm surges and heavy surf during the northeast storms of winter. (Years later, in the "Blizzard of '78," the wall was extensively damaged by erosion.) My uncle, who owned the barn, rented the upstairs apartment every summer to two retired nurses, Girty and Maggie. I visited them frequently when I was a little boy. I think they thought I was a "cute kid." The entrance stairway to the apartment led from the dirt yard to a large loft area on the second floor of the barn. Two kitchen windows overlooked the dirt yard and Main Street. A large loft area served as living and dining room combined. The thing that impressed me most was a large picture window facing the open ocean, which afforded a magnificent view. I loved that view, which once again got me thinking of the sea and imagining life in other lands. I knew even then that the sea was in my blood.

Girty and Maggie often sat on the porch in the morning, enjoying the view and sipping their morning coffee. They also enjoyed having a few cocktails in the afternoon, which they considered cocktail hour. Whenever I paid them a visit I was given a coke so that I could be a part of cocktail hour. One late summer afternoon, I was playing on the beach and becoming very thirsty when I saw them sitting on the porch with their cocktails in hand. I yelled, "Is it cocktail hour yet?" I think they felt embarrassed, since I was only six or seven years old at the time. Many of the people on the beach looked at me with surprise on their faces, but I didn't feel that I had done anything wrong. I preferred sailing and rowing with friends at the yacht club to doing the things my "townie" friends did. Many happy hours were spent on the waterfront, hanging out at the club with friends, fishing from the town float, or rowing my skiff around the harbor. My father owned a flat-bottomed plywood skiff built by a local boat-builder. The bow and stern were designed so that they barely made contact with the water's surface, thereby minimizing drag. The topsides were painted royal blue, and the inside was ocean gray. Most days during the summer, I could be found rowing, paddling, drifting, or sculling my skiff around the harbor. Although none of my friends would admit it, they knew it was the fastest skiff around. My friends couldn't come close to keeping up with me in a race, boat for boat.

On the Fourth of July we could choose between a watermelon-eating contest, a scavenger hunt, a sailing race, or the rowing race at the yacht club. The rowing race was the most popular choice for my friends and me. I remember in particular, at age twelve, defending my title as having the "fastest rowboat in the club." Several of my buddies and I anxiously lined up with our sterns touching the yacht club float. The objective was to row to the mouth of the harbor, pick up a floating balloon, and return to the starting point. I jumped off to a quick lead, but about a third of the way to the balloons, one of my oars jumped its oarlock, causing me to fall over backward. Both my legs went into the air, while both of my oars slid out of their oarlocks and into the water and began slowly drifting away from the skiff.

I was not deterred by this mishap, because I knew the speed potential of that rowboat and was determined not to be defeated! I paddled the skiff to each oar with my hands and recovered them. By this time, most of my competitors had passed me and were steadily moving away toward the balloons. Gradually, I reduced the distance to the lead boat, passed it, and retrieved my assigned balloon. This incident, complete with my legs and feet going into the air, is documented on a DVD that also shows me racing toward the finish line at full speed, no second-place boat in sight. I won the race hands down, thereby upholding my rowboat's reputation of being the fastest in the club! That day I was wearing heavy jeans, sneakers, and a white captain's hat with a black plastic visor and a nautical emblem embroidered on the hatband. I wore that hat every day for the longest time. Perhaps this was an early indication of a subconscious desire to become a captain. My friends often teased me by grabbing it and throwing it in the water.

I frequently watched an older man, named "Duffy" Blatchford, use a heavy rowboat to set and pull boat moorings, and wondered if this type of work would be a good way to earn some money using my prized rowboat. As a teenager I began doing mooring work, not realizing that it would put extra strain on the little boat. The added strain caused it to begin to leak and eventually become weakened. I still am not sure what became of that boat, but it lives on in my memories.

THE EARLY YEARS AT HOME

My father operated a Texaco gasoline station next to the old boat ramp in Dock Square. One day at work he saved the life of a child who had been locked inside a lobster car by his "buddies." A lobster car, used for storing lobsters until the price is favorable, is a large wooden crate weighted down with stones. This one was resting on the mudflats behind the station with the tide coming in. My father heard the boy screaming and went to investigate. When he opened the latch, he could not believe his eyes. That child grew to be an adult and has since passed on. He often reminded me of the day when my father saved his life.

Sometime later my father operated a small taxi business out of a large wooden garage, working from six in the morning to nine at night. Both the station and the cab business required long days, and he would arrive home totally exhausted. When he tried to close the gas station for the day, shutting down the pumps and turning off the lights, someone always seemed to drive in looking for a tank of gas. He could not refuse a customer, which often resulted in many late-night closings.

He worked so hard at his business that he had little time for family trips. On one family vacation to New Hampshire, we rented a small cottage on a lake. I enjoyed fishing from a small rowboat with my dad and my brother while we were there. I will not forget riding with my father to the Rockport train station to watch the steam locomotives approach the platform. The steam belching from around the wheels, and the sounds of the engine and whistle, left lasting impressions on me.

My father often stopped at Tuck's Drug Store to buy my mother a vanilla ice cream soda with strawberry ice cream. In those days customers sat on bar stools at the counter and watched every move as the soda water and syrup were mixed. There was another drugstore named Poole's at the other end of Main Street, where one could also purchase sodas and many other items. I knew most of the shopkeepers along Main Street and frequently stopped in to visit. Today the village pharmacies and hardware stores have all but disappeared from the American landscape.

A dirt path wound through a hilly cemetery from Front Beach and ended at Mill Lane, across the street from a friend's home. I recall walking hurriedly down the hill through the cemetery on that path after scout meetings, imagining dead bodies coming out of their graves. There is a large, half-round granite vault at the wall on Beach Street, where I thought dead bodies were stored until they were buried. I suppose now that it was used to store tools and other equipment. During the winter, after heavy snowfalls, my friends and I would ride sleds down the cemetery path and over the granite wall, crashing into the middle of Beach street. We thought nothing of the possibility of being hit by oncoming cars and being seriously injured or killed. We were kids, and kids don't think about those things.

Once I made a kite from materials found at home: large sticks, string, and plastic sheets. When I showed it to my sister Shirley's husband, Robert, he suggested that we fly it at the beach, where the wind was blowing hard out of the northeast. We got it off the ground and it soared higher and higher, requiring more and more string. Robert kept running to the store for more string, as I kept giving the kite slack. I never did locate that kite, and I wonder to this day where it finally came to rest after the string parted.

One of the neighborhood boys' favorite pastimes was having rock fights. I am not sure how this barbaric practice began, but I often found myself on the receiving end. My mom grew accustomed to seeing me arrive home with blood running down my face.

She always remained calm and comforted me as she treated the wounds. I was fortunate not to receive serious injuries from those incidents.

During my childhood, several large pleasure boats fished for tuna out of Rockport Harbor using harpoons, line, and kegs. The fish were landed at the end of Tuna Wharf and hoisted by the tail from a large wooden frame. They were carefully weighed before being shipped to their destination, which was often a foreign country. It was impressive to see them hanging from the heavy wooden gallows, but somewhat shocking because of all the blood and gore associated with the process. Boats still fish for tuna, and Japanese buyers will pay up to tens of thousands of dollars for prime fish, but it seems as though the average size of the fish has diminished since the days of my youth.

SECONDARY EDUCATION

Upon entering the seventh grade, I began to dislike the game of basketball. My brother was a star player on the high school basketball team, which had won the league championship four years in succession. This was amazing, because John had contracted polio as a young child. He had been required to wear leg braces for a long time, but he recovered to excel at baseball and basketball. I became a freshman three months after his graduation and was expected to follow in his footsteps, but I did not enjoy the game and felt pressure to perform at practices. The coach often criticized me for not doing well. After one especially disappointing practice, when my mom asked me how it had gone, I responded that I was going sailing in my turnabout to escape the pressure. I believe my parents realized how I felt and understood why I eventually quit the team. John and I had difficulty relating to one another during our teen years. He received most of my family's attention, making me feel left out.

I knew deep down, however, that my time would come to excel and make my family proud of me. I focused my attention on the sea and sea-related subjects in my spare time. Whenever I did a self-directed project, it related to the ocean and ships in some way. I often gazed out the classroom window, looking toward the horizon while thinking of boats, ships, and the sea when I should have been paying attention to the teacher. Our senior-year classes were small, ten students or fewer, which allowed us to receive much valued individual attention. Upon graduation from high school, I was accepted into Maine Maritime Academy. Had it not been for the advice given to me by my dedicated teachers, I would not have had the opportunity to attend college. I am especially grateful, given the poor effort that I had put into my high school education.

EARLY DAYS ON THE WATERFRONT

My friends and I spent hours rowing around the harbor, exploring under the docks while weaving our boats among the moss-covered pilings. Occasionally we rowed to the local fish pier and were given cooked lobster bodies. It was a treat to sit on the rocks while we sucked the tiny bits of meat from the creatures' legs and then pulled the bodies apart, devouring every last bit.

In 1953, two yacht club members purchased three small sailboats known as Turnabouts, which were designed for training young sailors. Five families became interested and ordered boats, which were delivered the following year. My father, noticing my excitement about these boats, asked me if I would like a new Turnabout. It seemed as though the winter of 1954 – 55 dragged on forever, as I waited first for my new boat to be delivered on Christmas Day and then for spring to come. I launched her early in the spring and christened her *Whirlwind*.

I spent many hours on the waters of Sandy Bay, learning about the weather and currents, watching the birds, exploring the islands and bays, and perfecting my sailing skills. On pleasant afternoons in the fall, I rushed home from school, changed clothes, and went to the yacht club. After grabbing my sail, lifejacket, and oars, I was ready to explore Sandy Bay once again. My mom visited an older couple in a nearby cottage almost every afternoon. Knowing that I would be anxious to sail after school, she always had a change of clothes ready so that I could go right to my boat. She said that

she didn't worry about me in the boat because she knew I was a capable sailor. When I rode my bicycle, however, she worried that I would fall and hurt myself. My father owned a motorboat, and he and my mother enjoyed motoring out to watch us kids race our sailboats. When he could only take a short break from his work, he and my mother enjoyed walking to the headlands and sitting on the rocks with their binoculars as they searched for the *Whirlwind*.

The local yacht clubs designated one day each year as "Chowder Day." We sailed or were towed to the host club, anchored, and feasted at the dock upon chowder, fresh doughnuts, and cheese. Once, as we approached the Annisquam Yacht Club anchorage, I cast our anchor and attached rode line, only to watch it scale across the water without sinking. Lacking the necessary weight of a chain leader, the buoyant line remained afloat. This was the hands-on approach to learning seamanship. We went out there and did it firsthand instead of learning about it from books. It was an effective means of learning as long as it did not result in disaster or embarrassment. After lunch, we returned to our respective boats to race in the afternoon. Upon crossing the finish line of the last

race, we sailed for home, often arriving after dark. Occasionally we fearless sailors mustered our courage and dared to toy with the elements. On one such day most of us sailed back to Rockport after the last race of Marblehead Race Week, a voyage of eight hours in a Turnabout, racing ahead of a squall the entire time. Those boats were so small that our legs locked, making it almost impossible to stand when it was time to disembark.

On another occasion, while we were being towed from Annisquam like a string of ducklings behind a mother mallard, the wind abruptly shifted into the northeast, leaving us a few hundred yards to windward of Halibut Point with the seas building rapidly. The height of the seas caused the towline to part, putting us in danger of being blown onto a lee shore. The surf breaking on the granite ledges to leeward was a sight to scare the stoutest mariner. As our boats drifted closer to the rocks, the more experienced among us concentrated on maintaining calm and order. Eventually the Coast Guard's 36-foot motor lifeboat arrived on the scene and took several of us in tow, while the yacht club committee boat towed the rest to safety. It was one of the scarier situations of my early sailing days.

I loved maneuvering my rowboat and sailboat and observing how the boats reacted to various wind and sea conditions. I would try to make my rowboat fast alongside other rowboats as if I was handling a tugboat and coming to the rescue of another craft in distress. I watched a television program about racing iceboats on a lake and became interested in how the principles of sail applied to a craft sliding upon an icy surface.

Thinking that I wanted to build an iceboat, I found a pair of old shoe skates and some scrap lumber and went to work. I removed the steel runners from the shoes and mounted them on blocks of wood, then mounted the blocks on T-shaped arms. The sails were sewn together from old white sheets, which had been obtained from my mother and father. After a few days I was ready to take my craft to a nearby pond for its shakedown cruise. Disappointingly, it only slid sideways because I had forgotten to sharpen the runners of the skates. Doing this would have allowed them to dig into the ice and prevent the craft from sliding to leeward. By the time I figured this out and had gotten around to sharpening the skate runners, the ice had melted. To the best of my knowledge, the remains of my experimental iceboat are still in the pond today.

I had always known that the sea was to play an important part in my life. My life's ambition, as quoted in my high school yearbook, was "To make a living on the sea in one way or another." A girlfriend, named Helga and I were given the title of most nautical. Most of my school projects were focused on the sea. Once, using a history of fishing schooners as a guide, Helga and I drew a picture of a fishing schooner using colored chalk. It remained on the blackboard of our sixth-grade classroom for several months. On most days as I left the house, my mom would ask where I was going and my reply was "down to the club." I couldn't wait to spend time with my "boat friends" and just be around the water.

One day I watched "Duffy" Blatchford single-handedly haul a Manchester I Boat out of the water using the old hand-crank derrick on the yacht club dock. He used large steel rollers and heavy timbers to move the boat and cradle into its winter storage location, completing the job in stages. He would painstakingly rig a block and tackle from a well-placed deadman in order to provide enough mechanical advantage to move the boat a few feet, then repeat the rigging from a new deadman location to complete the next segment. This man, it turned out, had a significant impact upon my professional life. I had a great deal of respect for him and all he knew about boats, seamanship, and sailing. One of his favorite sayings was, "Don't make excuses. Your friends don't need them and your enemies won't believe you anyway." When I began racing *Whirlwind,* I was reluctant to try my own strategies. He said, "I would never win races by following others." I listened, began planning my own race strategies, and my performance improved.

The club captain, named Arthur Swanson, was a kind, elderly man, very proud of his shiny black 1953 Chevrolet sedan, which he parked next to the club gate. One night a friend and I hoisted a rowboat to the top of the flagpole. I was there the next morning when he noticed it and said, "Hmm, I wonder how that got up there." We got his message and lowered it to the dock as soon as he went for coffee. On another occasion we found boxes of paper cups stored in the meeting room loft, and it seemed a good idea to take the stacks of cups from the boxes and throw them across the floor, forming a sea of paper cups. As we were perpetrating this prank, we heard him arrive in his car. We froze, knowing there was nowhere to go, as he entered the room. He stopped, turned, and looked up to see the two of us standing there with deer-in-the-headlights looks. He said, "I am going up to get a newspaper, and when I come back I want to see this cleaned up." Needless to say, it was done quickly. I will always remember him standing on the club dock with his white shirt, captain's hat, black trousers, and a cigar stub protruding from his mouth.

Arthur and his elderly friends gathered at the club every day in the spring and fall to play cribbage at long varnished tables that are still there. While they played cribbage, my friends and I sat by the fireplace, telling stories and watching the fire burning in the large granite fireplace. Just to be troublemakers, we took pieces of old lumber with nails protruding from their ends, heated them in the fire until the nails were red hot, and then pressed the nails into the floor, branding imprints that remain to this day.

During the summer following my high school graduation, I was in charge of the sailing program and filled in as dock manager. The club's several old floats were buoyed up by long, rusty, cylindrical steel pontoons that had to be chipped and painted each spring. I was the one designated for that dirty and labor-intensive job. My work at the club was the only job I held before attending college. I could have done more to ease the financial burden of my college education, but my dad felt strongly that I should not have to work as a teen.

Having so much time to myself allowed me to explore the local waters in my Turnabout unburdened by work schedules and other obligations. I think my dad was right in allowing me to avoid such pressures while I was maturing. He once told me that I would have more than enough time to work for the rest of my life, and there was no need to rush into it. So I spent most of my free daylight hours sailing my little boat, most often alone. I watched the currents swirling around lobster buoys in the area where we raced. This gave me a clear advantage over my friends when we were racing. I observed changes in the weather and noted the effects of those changes on the waters. I tried new sail adjustments and frequently retuned my boat's rigging to improve her performance.

The Turnabout sail inventory includes a small spinnaker. When this sail was full and pulling hard, the blunt bow pushed a lot of water when sailing downwind on a windy day. Because we were hesitant to fly our "chutes" in such conditions, there were days when we all maneuvered our boats prior to the start of a race, wondering whether one of our competitors would be the first to set his or her spinnaker. There was always one who was not afraid to set a spinnaker, which of course challenged the rest of us to follow suit. One year, at the end of Marblehead Race Week, my crew and

I finished the last race after losing our bailer overboard. With *Whirlwind* nearly plowing under the water from the force of the spinnaker, my crew and I sat on the transom, trying desperately to keep the bow above water and stay afloat. We finished the race in the nick of time, for immediately after crossing the line, the boat plowed under, broached, and capsized.

Occasionally a severe weather change would cause considerable damage to the shoreline and moored boats in the harbor. During the autumn we sailors were always aware of the possibility of hurricanes working their way up the coast. Although this was a rare occurrence, I can recall one hurricane that left its mark on our protected little harbor. On August 31, 1954, Hurricane Carol, packing winds of ninety miles per hour, caused extensive damage to boats, trees, and the shoreline. We watched from the yacht club porch as boats capsized and broke away from their moorings. A Lightning class sailboat capsized, and its mast punctured the side of a Star boat. It was exciting but also scary to be in the middle of all that.

Knowing what I now know about seamanship, I am surprised that more precautions had not been taken prior to Carol's arrival. Much of the damage could have been avoided if measures such as setting out extra anchors and hauling boats prior to the storm had been taken. Eleven days later, Hurricane Edna followed a path similar to Carol's but somewhat farther east, and Rockport was spared the worst of the storm. On that occasion people helped one another protect their boats and equipment prior to the storm's arrival. A fellow sea scout and I worked all night, helping club members during a similar storm when I was in high school. These efforts were later recognized at an award ceremony at the yacht club. Both of us shared the honor of being the member who had contributed the most toward the welfare of the club and its members that year.

SEA EXPLORERS

Becoming a member of the Rockport Sea Explorers (more commonly known as Sea Scouts) was a pivotal decision in my life. In order to advance through the ratings to the highest rank of Quartermaster it was necessary to learn many subjects related to the sea. These subjects included semaphore, piloting, navigation, knot tying and many more. I constructed a working sextant and hand lead line, using materials that were in my father's workshop. Learning the thirty-two cardinal and inter-cardinal headings on the compass rose was one of the more challenging tasks. Dr. J. Wain Baker, a scout leader, offered any interested scouts an opportunity to attend classes in celestial navigation. I took advantage of this offer and signed up right away. By successfully completing these classes I learned how to use a sextant to measure the angle of a heavenly body above the horizon. After taking observations of at least three stars, I became skilled at plotting lines of position.

I also learned how to signal using a flashing light. My father had learned flashing-light signals in Boy Scouts and helped me become proficient. After several weeks, he felt that I was ready to take the test. Chief Hale administered the test using a small plastic box containing a battery-powered light bulb that could be flashed on and off in the correct sequence. My first attempt proved unsuccessful, but after another week of practice I had made great strides and become quite proficient. Nevertheless, the second attempt was a washout once again. I finally passed on my third attempt and was convinced that I knew the code and would never forget it. I am sure my father would have had a talk with Chief Hale had I failed on the third attempt.

A regatta was held during the spring, giving scouts an opportunity to test their skills at rowing, knot tying, semaphore, flashing-light signaling, heaving a line, and tug of war. We camped from Friday evening to Sunday afternoon near a beach, sleeping in large tents. I remember waking up each morning to the tempting aroma of Chief Hale's breakfast of fried eggs, bacon, and home fries. My position on the surfboat rowing team was nearest the stern on the starboard side, known as the stroke position. It is the responsibility of the stroke oar to set the pace. Our boat was smaller and lighter than the Monomoy surfboat and was known as a Racepoint model. Both boats are rowed by eight scouts, four on each side, and steered by a coxswain. The oars are made of ash and are extremely heavy. The coxswain calls instructions as he steers the boat using a long sweep oar held in place by a large brass oarlock at the stern.

In order to prepare for the regatta competitions, we practiced rowing a three-mile course in Sandy Bay, usually in the evenings. After these practice sessions we'd dock at a wharf made of granite that had been quarried locally many years before. We'd walk through the woods to the quarries, strip down, and enjoy a refreshing swim. Our boat usually finished second to Gloucester, but on one occasion we defeated them in the Saturday race, only to lose the most important race on Sunday. The rowing crew was treated well, because rowing was the most prestigious event of the regatta. The Monomoy could be rigged for sailing but did not sail efficiently, due to its gaff rig and excessive hull weight. I was assigned to become familiar with the rig, so I became "Captain of the Monomoy." We won the sailing race in 1954 and were presented with a trophy consisting of a brass sailboat on a varnished wood base. This trophy occupies a special place in my office.

Winters were slow, with few scout events other than the regular Friday night meetings at the yacht club and a monthly fleet meeting for all the "ships" in our area. A scout organization is known as a ship and is assigned a specific name, usually the name of a famous ship. The fleet meetings consisted of a formation, meeting, and presentation of awards, followed by a dance. I was proud when my mom pinned the Quarter Master Medal on my uniform at one of these meetings. Quarter Master was the highest rating in Sea Exploring and was considered the equivalent of Eagle Scout in Boy Scouts. The Mariner Girl Scouts attended these meetings in order to provide partners with whom to dance, but we boys sat in chairs on the opposite side of the hall from the girls and were reluctant to ask them to dance. I dreaded "ladies' choice," because one of the girls would usually ask me to dance, and I was very self-conscious about dancing. Our ship leaders constantly chased us down and coaxed us to ask a girl to dance.

One winter the town selectmen asked the sea scouts to row Santa Claus to Front Beach. Rowing against a stiff northwest wind with the temperature ten to fifteen degrees below freezing was grueling. Santa disembarked as planned, and our boat returned to the yacht club float. The weather forecast called for a nor'easter that night, causing me concern that the boat might break loose and sustain serious damage on the rocks. I pleaded with my parents for permission to put out extra lines, but they would not allow me out of the house because I had come down with a severe cold. I contacted the skipper, and he agreed to rig several extra lines. The next morning, however, I discovered the boat hard aground and severely damaged. Ever since, I have assumed responsibility for the loss of that boat even though I could not get to it in time. I was never able to determine the final cause of the boat breaking loose. Scouts were given an opportunity to go on cruises if they achieved rating advancement throughout the year. I spent a week on a Boston pilot schooner in the vicinity of the Boston Light Ship. As a vessel approached the pilot station, a small boat was launched, carrying a ship pilot. The pilot boarded the ship by means of a rope ladder with wooden rungs—a Jacob's ladder. On another occasion I sailed from Gloucester Harbor on a freighter with a fellow scout and seven seamen, bound to ports along the coast of Newfoundland. For two weeks we visited ports where the only source of income was fishing and working in the local fish processing plants. In one instance we worked in the hold, carrying large boxes of frozen fish from the cargo net to the place of stowage. It was hard labor for one dollar an hour.

The scouts cruised once a year aboard some of the local yachts in Rockport. I was assigned to a large sloop called the *Jolly Buccaneer*. Once, after we'd departed from Rockport, the wind shifted to the northeast and commenced to blow. Most of the scouts on board became sick from the violent motion of the boat. I recall climbing out on the bowsprit to take in and furl the jibs as the bow pitched wildly into the seas. My feet were locked on the bobstay and my arms were wrapped around the bowsprit. I felt the bow diving into a large swell and knew instantly that I had to hang on tightly. My entire body was immersed in cold seawater, but I weathered the experience, and its memory lives on in my mind.

The scouts benefited from an excellent relationship with Coast Guard personnel at Straitsmouth Lifeboat Station. We spent hours hanging out, playing pool, and learning about seamanship. My grandfather had been stationed there for sixteen years, and the opportunity to frequent his one-time duty station had a special significance for me. Drills were held yearly to demonstrate the lifesaving device known as the breeches buoy. A shot line was fired by means of a line-throwing gun to a nearby mast. The scouts posed as shipwrecked sailors and climbed into the breeches. When all was ready, they rode down the line clinging to the slings. We realized that, had this been an actual shipwreck, we would have been under water in the surf most of the time. Still, this rescue device and associated equipment was responsible for saving hundreds of lives. We stood watch with the seamen in a tall radar tower and made sunset patrols aboard the motor lifeboat. As I write this I am building a model of that motor lifeboat, because it was the first large boat that I was given the opportunity to maneuver.

We had a small whaleboat with the engine amidships. A cord

led from the engine compartment to the coxswain's position in the stern. When the cord was pulled, a bell sounded, signifying to the engineman the required gear and throttle position. On meeting nights, a crew manned the whaleboat, equipped with a portable signal lamp, while another crew stood by in the meeting hall, which looked toward the sea. We practiced our signaling skills by sending messages between crews. Two fishing dories and an O class sailboat completed our fleet. On Sunday mornings, a crew of scouts loaded the whaleboat with Sunday newspapers and trash bags. Our mission was to collect visiting yachtsmen's trash and deliver the newspapers. Many were concerned when they saw us come alongside, fearing that we would crash into their boats, but our crews were well trained and there were no incidents. On weekends, the whaleboat was used to patrol the sailboat races. We looked forward to having the opportunity to rig a boat on the hip and tow it to safety. My Turnabout, *Whirlwind,* was used to demonstrate how the sea scouts rescued capsized crews. I capsized my boat off the beach and waited for the motor whaleboat to come to my assistance.

ADVANCED SAILBOAT RACING

During the 1954 North American Star Championship, I helped push empty trailers on the dock after each boat was launched. I had no idea that sixteen years later during the 1970 North American Star Championship, I would be dock manager, responsible for launching and hauling the same kind of boats. *Whirlwind* was sold by 1963 and I was searching for an opportunity to sail a larger, more challenging type of boat. The star-boats lined up on the dock seemed the likely choice for me to improve my racing skills. As I was standing on the yacht club porch one day, Paul Woodbury, the owner of a pink Star named *Flamingo IV* asked me if I would like to sail with him. Thus began a relationship that lasted through three seasons. The owner of *Flamingo IV*, a resourceful skipper, fashioned a wind pennant from a short piece of copper wire and a seagull feather. Whenever we sailed by a floating seagull feather, one of us would reach over the side and grab it. By the end of the summer, we had accumulated a substantial pile of feathers in the stern. We traveled to many clubs, racing in several important championships. In 1964 we competed in the Eastern Olympic Star Trials, finishing tenth. This entitled us to sail in the final round in Chicago at Jackson Park Yacht Club, where we finished eleventh overall. All contestants were given a silver tie tack in the shape of a star with the numerals sixty-four. Little did I know at the time that my future wife, Sally, was working at a bank, located nearby on Michigan Avenue.

Upon finishing a race, most skippers would turn their boats over to their crews, who then competed to see who would arrive first at the hoist. Stars were dry sailed, meaning that they were pulled out of the water after each race. We all liked to be first out of the water so that we could be early at the social events following the race. These informal races to the hoist were beneficial to me because my skipper watched me closely, always commenting in a constructive way on my sailing skills. My skipper enjoyed racing on the edge, often maneuvering us into precarious positions. During one race we approached the weather mark on the port tack, fouling another boat. We were protested out of the race, causing us to lose the series. I tried to make my testimony as favorable as possible at the protest hearing, but we were wrong.

During Eastern Point Chowder Day, I borrowed a friend's Star. It was not very competitive due to its age and condition, but I wanted to sail it for the experience of skippering. We started the race and had rounded the course several times when a thick fog set in. I had noted the wind direction and the time required on each tack between the leeward and windward marks, so we sailed the final windward leg with timed tacks. Just as I was beginning to doubt myself, the finish mark and committee boat materialized from the fog dead ahead. We had been dead last when the fog had set in, yet when we crossed the finish line, the cannon sounded. I said to my crew, "Damn, we won the race!" Several of my competitors had become lost and never did find the finish line. One sailed over a mile off course before realizing his error. This experience boosted my self-confidence and emphasized the importance of never giving up.

A SAILING LESSON

One day a girl in whom I had been interested for some time told me that she had purchased a small catboat. She wondered if I would sail with her to Annisquam, and race in the Chowder Day race. She wanted me to give her suggestions as to the best way to sail it. How could I turn down such a perfect opportunity to impress her with my knowledge and prowess with sailing and to be with her for the day? We sailed to Annisquam in the morning, intending to anchor off the dock. We were to have our chowder, race, and then sail back to Rockport following the race. She had brought her portable radio, wrapping it in a plastic bag to keep it dry. As we sailed past Lanesville I put my arm around her. I could not easily handle the tiller and tend the mainsheet with my one free arm, so I secured the mainsheet on the centerboard cleat. When we tacked, we did not bother to change our weights to the weather side. The wind was light, and I was casual about the danger of heeling and capsizing. Then, suddenly, the wind began to increase, causing us to heel sharply. From our seats on the lee side it was difficult to reach up to the centerboard trunk in order to release the mainsheet, and the next thing we knew, the boat was capsizing. We slid into the water backwards, and when I came up I could not see her anywhere. Frightened, I searched frantically for her, only to find her under the sail in a small air pocket.

The current had caused us to drift to a point off the club dock, in plain view of all those having their chowder on the dock.

The bag containing the radio had sufficient air in it to keep it afloat, and the music was still playing. We bailed the boat and obtained a ride to our homes in Rockport for some dry clothes, and returned for the long awaited clam chowder. Still another mishap was ahead after lunch, however. Prior to the start of the race, I misread the course letters on the committee boat, causing us to head for the wrong downwind mark. At that point we sailed for Rockport, calling it quits. Although the sailing lesson was a bust and turned out to be considerably embarrassing for me, all was not lost. We had an enjoyable moonlit sail home.

MANCHESTER 18-FOOT CLASS

Early in the twentieth century, several wealthy yachtsmen commissioned the design of a class of sailboats known as the Manchester Eighteens. Sailboat handicapping rules of that day penalized waterline length but not length on deck, and the ongoing effort to beat the rules resulted in boats with long, overhanging bows and long counter sterns. The Manchester Eighteens were 18 feet long on the waterline and approximately 30 feet overall. Long, low, graceful, and beautiful, when these boats heeled, their speeds increased along with their effective waterline lengths. Unlike most modern sailboats, therefore, they performed best when heeled.

The boats were sailed by professional captains while the owners placed bets on which boat would win. The fleet grew smaller in number as the years passed, due to normal wear and tear on wooden boats that were sailed hard. Only six of the boats remained in Rockport when I was a child, and by the time I passed into my teen years and attended high school, the number had decreased to five. Following my graduation from Maine Maritime Academy I purchased one of these, named *Nipper*, and raced it for two years. At the time, I was at sea for about two-thirds of each year, and it became a burden to maintain an aged wooden boat with its constant demands for tender loving care. I hated to part with *Nipper*, but it seemed to be the best thing for me to do at the time.

Each Manchester Eighteen was placed on a wooden cradle

and moved into a winter storage location with the aid of block and tackle. The long, overhanging bow and stern had to be supported by timbers, which were wedged into place. This procedure caused uneven stresses upon the hulls, which resulted in gradual changes of shape over time. The original sails had been made of cotton and had stretched substantially over time. It was necessary to dry them thoroughly following a rain to prevent the formation of mildew. Later, Dacron became the material of choice, thereby easing the maintenance burden. Some boats had newer Dacron sails, but others still sailed with their baggy cotton canvas. Such factors resulted in a fleet of boats of markedly varying speed potentials. *Nipper* had been well maintained over the years, making it the fastest boat in the fleet.

The wood hulls dried during the winter, causing the planks to shrink and the seams to open, sometimes so much that daylight could pass through. We were obliged to keep a stream of water running into the hull for a week before launching in order to swell the planking. The launching was done with the boat in slings overnight under the derrick, to prevent it from filling with water and sinking at the dock. The crews pumped steadily with hand pumps during the races to keep the water level under control. We were greatly relieved when the automatic bilge pump was invented. In later years the Manchester Eighteens became more commonly known as I Boats. The mast was shaped with a permanent bend near the top, allowing more overall sail area. This was a method used to allow for the maximum sail area, while maintaining the mast at a specific height required by class rules.

Races were held in Sandy Bay each Saturday and Sunday of the summer. After the races, when the other fleets had secured their boats and headed home, the I Boat crews usually gathered on one boat and socialized. Some of us chose to jump into the water to cool off on extremely warm days. There was a wooden bucket on board *Nipper* labeled "4 U 2 P," and it was used often. Each boat owner had a rowboat for transportation to and from the mooring. Some of those rows to the dock were wet, with several people crammed into a little rowboat. If one of us leaned to one side it was easy for the boat to fill with water leaving us all floundering around in the water. Sally and I came to call the summer we met "the Super Summer of '70," and *Nipper* played an important role in that summer.

PART TWO

THE PROFESSIONAL YEARS

MAINE MARITIME ACADEMY

Castine, Maine, situated on the shore of a small inlet on Penobscot Bay, is one of the oldest towns in North America. France, Holland, England, and colonial America all occupied Castine at least once after its initial settlement. Several well-preserved fortifications remain today. Fort George, consisting of a large, flat plot of ground surrounded by dirt redoubts, is located high on the shore near the Maine Maritime Academy. Including MMA, there are five state-operated post-secondary maritime-training schools in the country, and one operated by the federal Government. Students graduating at the time I attended could acquire a United States Coast Guard license as Third Assistant Engineer or Third Mate—that is to say, you could be an engineer or a deck officer.

While preparing for high school graduation, I learned of Maine Maritime Academy from a friend and decided that a career at sea was for me. After submitting the necessary application forms and waiting for what seemed like months, I was accepted. I was excited, albeit somewhat apprehensive, that the first step had been taken to set me on course for a seagoing career. My friend offered the following advice prior to my reporting date: "Keep your mouth shut, keep it straight ahead, and do as you are told." This advice was well taken and served me in good stead for the four years that I was in attendance. I was unaware of what lay ahead on that August day that I reported for the first time.

For the initial six weeks of our freshman year, we were subjected to a rigorous indoctrination period during which our heads were shaved and we were exposed to abusive insults designed to lower all of us to the same psychological level. The indoctrination included running, push-ups, marching, and other efforts intended to whip us all into excellent physical condition. Our uniforms, books, and other supplies were issued at the ship's store, situated in a tiny area in the basement of a brick classroom building. Following the issuance of uniforms and other essential equipment, we marched down the hill for the first time, dropping items and being verbally harassed along the way. Looking ahead as I marched down the hill, I saw a huge ship moored to a dock on the waterfront. This was an ex-Navy hospital ship on loan to the academy from the United States Government. I learned that this ship would be our home for the entire first year. The presence of a large seagoing vessel amidst the peaceful wooded surroundings was a totally unexpected sight. Our platoon leader screamed insults and constantly criticized our lack of marching skills all the way to the waterfront.

We were told that we would learn the history of Fort George during the first week of indoctrination. During the next several weeks we learned a small amount of history but did receive an excessive amount of physical and verbal abuse in "the fort." Our days drilling in the fort were extremely tiring and wearing. If we fell out of step while drilling we were ordered to do push-ups or run around the parade grounds. All the while we were made to feel as though we were the lowest beings on earth. One hot summer day at the fort, my nose began to bleed profusely. I let the blood run down upon my new uniform shirt and pants and then reported it to the officer in charge. He immediately ordered me to report to sickbay. This was one way to avoid marching, but it ruined my uniform. No cadet who has endured the rigors of indoctrination will forget the long and grueling "duck walk" up "agony hill" or those exhausting days drilling for hours in "The Fort."

We freshmen, known as Mugs during the first year, were

required to memorize specific responses to questions asked by upperclassmen. If an upperclassman passed me in a hallway, I was to say, "By your leave sir," and if I met an upperclassman I would say, "Excuse me sir." When upperclassmen asked me a question, I was allowed to respond with "Yes sir," "No sir," "No excuse sir," or "I'll find out sir"—answers I had many occasions to use throughout my career. When passing an upperclassman in a hallway, I was required to "hit a brace." This meant that I quickly turned ninety degrees and slammed my back against the wall while pulling my stomach in as tight as possible and lowering my chin to touch my chest. I was to focus my eyes upon a point directly ahead and not look in any other direction.

If I wished to speak to an upperclassman, the question had to be prefaced with, "Fourth Classman Grimes requests permission to speak, sir." When the question, "Mr., how long have you been sailing" was put to me, I was required to reply, "All me blooming life, sir. Me father was King Neptune. Me mother was a mermaid. I was born on the crest of a wave and rocked in the cradle of the deep. My eyes are stars. My teeth are spars. My hair is hemp and seaweed. When I spits, I spit tars. I'se tough, I is, I am, I are, sir!" If this answer was not given with emphasis and recited entirely correctly, the penalty was several hours of extra duty.

There were times when I doubted the wisdom of my decision to attend Maine Maritime Academy. Whenever this occurred, I would repeat to myself the mantra, "You know why you are here," and I was able to go on. To prepare for daily uniform inspections, I had to brush lint from my uniform, shine the brass buckle on my belt, and spit shine my shoes. I was reduced to sneaking around during the night in order to find a place to shine my shoes for the next day's inspection. Even though I did not smoke, I was compelled to have a few packs of cigarettes always on my person. If an upperclassman asked me for a cigarette, I could avoid further harassment by having one easily accessible. If I could not produce a cigarette, I was forced to do push-ups or perform extra duty. It did not take long to learn that lesson.

I was required to do mess duty at regular intervals during the first year. This included standing by the regimental officers' meal table and fetching whatever they desired. One of their favorite forms of harassment was to require me to peel them an onion. When I returned with the sliced onion, the slicing of which had brought me to tears, the senior would usually say, "I don't want that, Mug. Throw it in the garbage."

When my classmates and I were having our meal in the mess deck, the words "food fight" followed by a specific time were often passed from table to table. When this time showed on the clock, all hell would break loose as potatoes and other items of food began hurtling through the air. This type of pastime was good for us, because it helped to relieve the rigors of academy life.

One of a Mug's watch-standing duties was making regular rounds of the buildings and grounds to guard against the possibility of a fire. We carried a flashlight and a time clock, which was used to record each station stop. We were told to make these rounds as fast as possible, which seemed to defeat the purpose of being alert.

I fell on the pavement one night, ruining my uniform and injuring a knee, but I was shown little compassion by my watch officer upon my return to the quarterdeck.

We were also required to make clock rounds on board the training ship. The ex-hospital ship was fitted with a morgue, in which the bodies of dead World War II servicemen had once been kept until such time as they could be removed ashore. There was a key station just outside the morgue door and next to no lighting in the area. As I was making my rounds one evening, I approached the key station and prepared to insert the key into the clock when I heard moaning from inside the morgue! I do not believe in ghosts, but I distinctly heard this voice, and the adrenalin instantly flooded my body. I quickly punched the key into the clock and almost ran up the ladder to get out of the vicinity. When I reported what I had heard, I was laughed off the quarterdeck by the upperclassmen. I learned later that this was part of the ritual that all freshmen went through on their first year.

I often tried to imagine what life on this ship had been like during wartime. It is reported that the ship was attacked by kamikaze warplanes on several occasions. Several nurses had been killed during one such attack. There were small cells with barred doors where those who had broken down under the stress of warfare had once been confined.

I slept on one of thirty steel pipe racks that were stacked two high in a crowded compartment. Each of us was required to stow our gear into one small locker. None of us will forget the "junk on the bunk" inspections, when a senior would suddenly burst into the compartment yelling, "Ok, gentlemen, junk on the bunk!" Upon hearing this command, each of us struggled to arrange our gear on our bunks for inspection. It was a chaotic experience, as we bumped into one another, dropping gear everywhere. Our bunks were often far from our lockers, which made it more confusing. Every item of clothing was required to be properly rolled, stopped, and stenciled with our names. My bunk was made so tightly that a quarter would bounce if it were dropped on the blanket. Each bunk was required to be made four and eight, meaning that the distance was eight inches from the head end of the mattress to the point where the sheet was folded back. The folded portion of the sheet was required to measure four inches. These measurements were checked by upperclassmen with a ruler at each inspection.

It was difficult to find study time uninterrupted by the harassment of upperclassmen. I often hitched rides to the nearby town of Bucksport on weekends and checked into a local motel just to catch up on my studies and escape the apprehension of being told to do something by upperclassmen. My classmates and I found hiding spots throughout the ship for the weekends that we had to remain on campus doing duty. There was a difference between the hazing done by upperclassmen during indoctrination and the tension-relieving hazing experienced later. Once I was ordered to wrap my head in toilet paper and then proceed to each of the seniors' rooms, one at a time. I would request permission to enter each room, and after being told rather abruptly to enter, I would ask for permission to speak. I then uttered, "Fourth Classman Grimes is a s…t head, sir!" Reflecting back on this experience, I realize that it did relieve the tension and give me something to laugh at.

There is one type of hazing that can be physically harmful and is not allowed at Maine Maritime Academy. The midshipmen make a cruise each year in order to acquire seagoing experience in preparation for the issuance of a Third Officer License. During the cruise, the time is divided into three sections: Deck, Engine, and Steward. During the engine third of my freshman cruise, while I was standing fireman watch in front of one of the boilers, a senior ordered me to wire brush the hot steel deck plates by hand while kneeling. I tried to do so, but felt the skin burning on my knees. I changed position so that I would not become burned and was ordered once again to kneel. I decided that it was not worth physically harming myself and that it was time to stand up to this senior. I told him that his orders constituted physical hazing and that the practice was not allowed at the academy. I suggested that he rescind his order or go with me to meet with the master of the vessel to explain his actions. I knew that acting as I had could possibly have led to my being hazed so badly that I would be forced to leave the academy. Later in the spring I asked one of the seniors in the academy yacht club whether the word had been passed to haze me out of the school. When he replied that it had been passed, I asked why the seniors had not complied. My intuition proved to be accurate when he said that no one in the class liked this individual, so the word was ignored.

Upon completion of the indoctrination period, I was permitted to wear my dress uniform for the first time on weekend liberty. I recall proudly hitchhiking home in my dress blues to have my friends and family see me in my uniform. I encountered some interesting characters while hitching. There was the Belfast chicken farmer who said as I approached his pickup truck, "I'm not going too far, but maybe I can help a little." I did not take into consideration the chicken feathers all over the cab of the truck, and I was a long while removing those feathers from my dress blues. As I walked up to one car, the driver said, "I hope you don't mind my being a little nervous, but I just tried to kill my wife." Needless to say, I turned down that ride immediately. After riding for several miles with a man on the Maine Turnpike, he asked me if I had ever had sex with a man. I stated that I was not interested and suggested that he should stop the car and let me out immediately. I fell asleep once while riding on the Maine Turnpike but was awakened by a sensation of speed. I glanced at the odometer to find that it was reading 120 miles per hour. A state police officer stopped the car and arrested the driver at the next tollbooth, telling me to continue on my way the best way possible. One afternoon a state trooper picked me up between Augusta and Bucksport, but instead of issuing me a citation for hitchhiking, he drove me to a restaurant in Bucksport, treated me to a cup of coffee, and passed me along to another trooper who drove me to the academy. My classmates wondered why I was riding in a state police car, and I kept them guessing.

During my first cruise to Bermuda, Barbados, and Brazil,

I was indoctrinated into King Neptune's Realm. On the evening before the vessel crossed the equator, we "pollywogs" were allowed to seek out as many "shellbacks" as possible and take them into custody. A "pollywog" has never crossed the equator, and a "shellback" has been across at least once. We captured our physics instructor, and locked him inside one of the cells, which had been used to isolate those with mental illness during World War II. All of us enjoyed taunting him and spraying shaving cream on his face during his confinement. The storekeeper barricaded himself in the stores locker in order to avoid being captured by the pollywogs, but lost the battle in the end. Several others were captured and harassed, but they knew they would get even with the pollywogs the next day during the indoctrination ceremony for crossing the equator.

Just prior to crossing the equator, a proclamation was read by a representative of King Neptune's court, followed by the indoctrination ceremony. Pollywogs were required to wear their shirts backwards so as to restrict the movement of their arms, and each pollywog was then blindfolded and made to kiss the Royal Baby's belly, which had been smeared with grease and all manner of gross concoctions. The cook then sprayed a vile-tasting liquid into each pollywog's mouth, and we were herded to the mouth of a canvas tunnel running at a right angle to the ship's centerline. As each pollywog knelt to crawl through this tunnel, he felt a jet of water hitting him from behind with the force of a fire hose. I felt apprehensive, because I wasn't certain that someone was at the other end to stop me from shooting over the side of the ship. As I exited the tunnel, I felt someone grab my hair and pull my head up abruptly. He asked if I had enjoyed the events of the previous evening, to which I replied enthusiastically, "Yes Sir!" He then struck me several times from behind with a length of rubber hose, causing such intense pain that I was sore for a week. It was the physics instructor getting his revenge. The pollywogs were then processed by last name in alphabetical order. As each of us completed his indoctrination, he was allowed to take part with the shellbacks. Those whose names began with letters toward the end of the alphabet received much more punishment. I was glad that my surname was Grimes, not a name beginning with a letter toward the end of the alphabet. I enjoyed the experience and still have the certificate proving me a "Shellback."

Mugs stood lookout on the stern of the ship, which offered another opportunity for harassment by upperclassmen. The stern lookout station was adjacent to the movie theater on the ship's fantail, and frequently a senior would taunt the Mug on stern lookout while waiting for the movie to begin. The Mug would have to ignore the taunts, or else the senior might accost him later and make him do extra duty or run errands.

During July and August, half the student body worked maintenance for thirty days while the rest were on liberty. I belonged to the academy yacht club, serving as an officer each year. The club maintained two cruising sloops, which participated in local overnight races to nearby islands. Several small racing sloops for intercollegiate competition were added to the fleet during my senior year.

After one year, each student chose Deck or Engine as his course of study until graduation. Deck students trained to become licensed deck officers, and Engine students prepared for a career as licensed engineers. I was certain from the day I entered the academy that I was going to pursue the Deck course. During my second summer at the academy, the hospital ship was to be delivered to Beaumont, Texas, to be scrapped. The school was going through a transition from a three- to a four-year curriculum. The seniors had graduated in June, and the sophomore class was to deliver the ship to Texas. This left my class with the run of the school for two months, during which I qualified to skipper the two sloops. When the upperclassmen returned with the new training ship (Ex: SS *Ancon)* they were not pleased to learn that several of us had qualified on the sailboats.

The *Ancon* was a combined cargo and passenger ship operated by the United States government to transport cargo, employees, and their dependents between the ports of New York and Cristobal, Panama. The accommodations were a big improvement over the compartment living on board the old hospital ship. The main dining area amidships consisted of a spacious carpeted room with large glass cases containing live plants. During the annual cruise, the freshmen lived in the old crew quarters aft and the upperclassmen in the former passenger quarters forward.

In January of my sophomore year, the ship departed Penobscot Bay for several East Coast ports and the Panama Canal, San Diego, and San Francisco. Movies were shown each evening to any midshipmen not standing watch, sleeping, or otherwise engaged. On our first night out the movie was "The Last Voyage," and in view of subsequent events, I wonder if that was an omen. During the evening of our third day at sea, a fire ignited inside the smokestack. Upon later investigation the cause was found to be spontaneous combustion in a pile of oily rags that had been improperly stowed.

The passage to the Panama Canal and then to San Diego went without incident, and during our five-day stay in San Diego, many midshipmen became friends with naval personnel on station nearby. When the ship departed for San Francisco, all hands stood at attention along the rails in full dress uniform. The band played, and colors were dipped in salute to naval vessels passed in the channel. I was having lunch in the main dining room following departure when I noticed smoke seeping from the perimeters of the space. I heard the general alarm, followed by an announcement on the loud speaker that this was not a drill and that all hands were to proceed to their previously assigned fire and emergency stations. My station was at the stern deckhouse, as far aft as one could go on the ship, and I proceeded there. I was sure the problem was in the engine room, and I felt the urge to go there and offer assistance, but the station bill assignments were to be followed at all times. There were so many of us on board that the assignments had to be well spread about the ship.

A gasket in the main steam line had ruptured, causing high-pressure steam to escape into the machinery area. The condensing steam caused a short circuit in the main electrical board, which resulted in our second fire of the cruise. One midshipmen standing near the point of rupture miraculously escaped injury. After the fire was extinguished, the vessel drifted without power for several hours in the vicinity of the sea buoy while negotiations took place between vessel and shore personnel to determine how the ship would be towed to port for repairs. Many of the naval personnel who had saluted us on the way out noticed that we had returned to port on the following day and probably wondered about the circumstances. For the next several weeks the vessel was laid up in a shipyard undergoing repairs, which consumed so much time that it became necessary for us to proceed directly back to the East Coast.

Today each midshipman goes to sea on board a United States merchant ship during one year and makes a cruise on the training ship each of the other three years. This enables students to gain real-life experience, as compared with receiving limited practical shipboard opportunities on the academy training ship. The only practical cargo-handling experience I received was during one summer when it was necessary to load large granite blocks into the lower holds of the training ship and secure them as permanent ballast. When I attended the academy, the system of shipping out as a cadet had not yet been inaugurated. I would have benefited greatly from a year of practical cargo-handling experience.

I held the rating of First Class Petty Officer for one year and lived in the freshman dormitory with a classmate who held a similar rating. Our responsibilities included maintaining discipline and providing counseling. To relieve tension among the beleaguered mugs, my roommate and I decided to organize a group of them into a raiding party. We had an apple press in the room and thought it would be a cool idea to make apple cider, with the apples to come from a tree in the admiral's backyard. Mustering a dozen Mugs, we gave them baskets and sent them on their mission. Returning with full baskets, they had to climb two flights of stairs to reach our room. One of the Mugs tripped on the top floor landing and spilled a basket of apples, sending them bouncing down the stairs to the ground floor. The officer on duty failed to notice a thing out of the ordinary, which amazes me to this day. We squeezed the apples and stored the juice in bottles. Neither my roommate nor I had any knowledge of the use of preservatives in this process, so the juice continued to ferment until we broke out the bottles during the holiday season. Having realized that we had produced almost pure alcohol, a handful of us consumed a good portion of the "cider" and had a good time.

One afternoon in 1963, as we were preparing for inspection, a midshipman coming down the hallway called out that President Kennedy had been shot. Everyone was stunned by the news, and silence took over as we attempted to digest it. I traveled home to Rockport for the weekend to find everyone in a state of shock. On Sunday, as I waited for a classmate to pick me up for the ride back to school, I watched on television as law enforcement officials escorted the president's accused assassin, Lee Harvey Oswald, through the basement of a building. Suddenly a man emerged from the crowd wearing a black dress hat and black overcoat, and it was immediately clear that something was going terribly wrong. He approached Oswald face to face, and suddenly Oswald grimaced in pain, having been shot in the midsection. No one who witnessed those events can forget when, glued to our televisions, we tried to comprehend what was happening to America.

I found the applied maritime subjects easier to understand than the academic subjects such as calculus and physics, which I passed by the skin of my teeth. This did not make me feel too badly, however, because an understanding of the professional subjects was essential for a career at sea. The material that I had learned in Sea Scouts was a huge benefit to me in these subjects.

I will always remember those instructors at the academy who played such an important part in preparing me for a life at sea. There was Captain Philbrook, known to us as "the Fidd," who taught us the nautical rules of the road. Lieutenant Wibby taught physics, a subject many of us labored at for hours each night. Captain "Jack" Kennaday taught astronomy, math, and the literature of the sea. Captain John Fordan passed on much valued knowledge during cargo class. Bos'n Lunt, the ship's bos'n, spoke with a thick Maine accent and was in charge of maintaining the ship. Stan Trott, the storekeeper, issued painting gear during the cruises. Commander Gray, also known as "Buffy," was in charge of the waterfront, and who could forget Captain Terry, also known as the "Baron?"

The Fidd was famous for his surprise Monday morning one question quizzes that very often required a large amount of writing. No partial credit was given; your grade was either a 100 or a 0. When students complained about the unfairness of these quizzes, he would reply, "I've got mine," meaning that if we did it his way we would get our licenses. Those quizzes were painful in the beginning, but they conditioned us to be ready for anything, and it paid off. When we took the Coast Guard exam for license qualification, most of us received 100%.

"Delta" Wibby used Greek letters constantly to demonstrate the formulas and principles of physics. I became extremely confused in that class and passed the term with little breathing room. I have always had considerable difficulty understanding subjects that seemed more abstract.

Captain Jack was faculty advisor to the academy yacht club and respected by all. He was profoundly interested in teaching astronomy and enjoyed having us draw diagrams of heavenly bodies on the plane of the celestial meridian. He designed an astronomy laboratory in the attic of Dismukes Hall in order to demonstrate the location of the major constellations, planets, and stars. One summer afternoon, Captain Jack informed me that he wished to take his daughter and some guests for a sail on the academy sloop, *Diana,* and he asked me to sail the boat. I docked at the town dock with the aid of a classmate and rigged the sails. When our guests had boarded and it was time to get underway, I ordered my crew to raise the jib, only to find to my embarrassment that he had put the jib on upside down. I had wanted to impress

Captain Jack by sailing away from the dock. It was an early lesson to check the work of those in my charge.

Captain John held a wealth of knowledge gained from years of seagoing experience, mostly on ships carrying bananas. We learned much practical knowledge about the hazards that could be encountered by longshoremen and ship personnel while loading. During one of the cruises, Captain John and I stood on the bridge wing on a clear, sunny day. He reached his hand into the air, flexing his fingers in and out, and said, "It's going to come in thick tonight." Sure enough, by midnight I heard the ship's whistle sounding the fog signal. There was no end to the practical knowledge that I gained from him.

Bos'n Lunt was in charge of ship maintenance. He was an old salt whose favorite saying to me was, "Goddamn her Grimes, what are you doing?" I learned a great deal about seamanship from him. On the summer after we received the new training ship, I was on a crew assigned to refinish the handrails on the upper decks. Because the ship had carried passengers as well as cargo, she was fitted with many wooden rails, all in very bad condition. Bos'n Lunt was a yachtsman at heart and took great pride in those rails, and by the end of the summer we had them looking like new.

Stan Trott was in charge of paint, paintbrushes, and associated supplies. Whenever I was sent to his stores locker in search of paint or brushes for an assigned job, I would ask, "Hey Stan, do you have any black paint?" The reply was almost always "I got the paint if you got the brushes!" He hated to part with paintbrushes.

Commander Buffy was an old salt in charge of maintenance on the waterfront. During one summer maintenance period, he told me to go over to the town dock, pick up a rowboat, and row it to the outboard side of the training ship. As I rowed around the ship's stem, he yelled in his heavy Maine accent, "Goddamn, Grimes, where did you learn to feather your oars?" This surprised me, because I thought everyone feathered their oars when they rowed.

The Baron taught celestial and coastal navigation. When his

class began, the section leader would always call out, "Attention on deck!," and the Baron would then slowly walk across the room with a cigarette in one hand and a cup of coffee in the other, saying, "Gentlemen, take this down." He would then read off the particulars of a navigation problem, which we were expected to record on blank sheets of paper and solve. His problems were written on dog-eared, wrinkled, old index cards and had been used years ago before when he ran his own navigation school in Boston. One day he taught us the methods of taking horizontal sextant angles with a sextant, and I just could not seem to get it. He became more and more frustrated with me as time passed. I did eventually understand it, but only after much embarrassment and damage to my pride.

One day as the Baron was giving us the results of the last quiz, he said, "I am happy to say that Mr. Grimes does not have a 4.0." He knew that another classmate and I had been having an informal contest to see how many perfect scores we could earn in a row. I think the record was ten to that point. It was a friendly rivalry, because this student was one of my best friends and we got along very well.

During our senior class banquet, we were all having a great time, having put the stress of final exams and Coast Guard exams behind us. I tapped my knife on a glass and said, "I would like to propose a toast to the Baron, Ace Navigator." All hands gave a great cheer. His response was, "And I would like to return Mr. Grimes' toast, to Midshipman Grimes, who finally learned to take a horizontal sextant angle."

We joke in these later years about those able instructors, but because of their efforts, we learned the material and learned it well. My sincere gratitude goes to all of those at Maine Maritime Academy who challenged me to excel and do my absolute best. My years as a student at MMA were some of the best of my life. I carry many fond memories of those times.

THE MERCHANT MARINE LICENSE PROCESS

In 1965, the process for obtaining an officer's license in the United States Merchant Marine consisted of a series of examinations coupled with experience requirements between each grade. The examinations were of the essay type. The applicant picked an index card from a box and returned to his seat and began writing his response essays on a lined, yellow legal pad. If he knew the answers to the questions, he felt a sense of relief. An advantage of this system was that partial credit could be given if some parts of the answer were missing. It was this type of examination that each of us faced prior to taking final exams for graduation. We had to pass the Coast Guard exams or we were not allowed to take our finals. Those two weeks were the most difficult that I have faced in my academic career. Thanks to the excellent preparation I had received from my instructors, however, I passed all of the exams with no problem and was ready to begin the next phase of my life voyage.

The license examination system has changed substantially since 1965. Now the examinations have a multiple-choice format, making them faster both to take and to correct but eliminating the possibilities for partial credit. The exams are corrected by a central facility, leaving no room for individual consideration by the examiner. The questions are often tricky and difficult to answer.

MY NEXT VOYAGE BEGINS

Shortly before I completed my studies at Maine Maritime Academy, a representative from American Export-Isbrandtsen Steamship Lines came to the academy to speak with graduating deck students. After briefing us on company benefits and giving us a description of company operations, he informed us that we could be on board a ship in less than a week if we chose to be employed with his company. In 1965, crews were urgently needed to operate break-bulk cargo vessels supplying the military forces in Vietnam. At this time the military draft was a very real factor in a young man's life, and I was being offered the option of satisfying my military obligation by serving on board a merchant ship for a minimum of six years. Several of my friends opted to give up their citizenships and live in Canada rather than face the military draft and serve in a war they did not support. I elected to sign on with AEIL.

A few days following graduation, I traveled to Logan Airport in Boston and boarded a shuttle jet destined for Newark, New Jersey and the beginning of a new career. At that time there was no check-in required for tickets. Passengers boarded the plane, found a satisfactory seat, and settled in. Just after take-off the flight attendant walked down the aisle and collected the fare in cash. ($35.00 at that time) After collecting my fare, the flight attendant asked me if I would like a magazine. Without realizing the possible implications of what I was about to say, I asked her if she had any life. (Life Magazine) Her response was one that, I dare say, we would not hear today. She replied, "I have plenty of life, how about you"? This exchange lightened up the tension that I felt as I headed for a new and relatively unknown situation. Upon locating the company headquarters in Hoboken, I found that the first step in the hiring process was to obtain a physical examination with a company doctor whose office was in Greenwich Village. Having been raised in a small New England town, I had never ridden a subway before; my first ride was from New Jersey to Manhattan. The cursory nature of the examination surprised me; I was not required to undergo an eye or hearing test, nor was I asked to submit to any X-rays.

After returning to company headquarters with my physical examination results, I was given a reservation at the Continental Hotel—which sounded like a fancy five-star accommodation— where I would stay while awaiting my first shipboard assignment." Directly across the street from the company piers, I peered up a side street to spot an old rickety sign suspended by a rusting chain and bearing the name, Continental Hotel. This was the first disappointment of my new adventure. As I climbed several steps to the front door, I could not help noticing the garbage in the alleyways and the homeless people milling about.

After climbing four flights of dirty stairs surrounded by very dirty walls, I entered my new temporary quarters. My eye was immediately drawn to a bare light bulb hanging from the center of the ceiling at the end of a black electrical cord. As I attempted to adjust to this unexpected decor, I noticed several good-sized cockroaches crawling on the walls. I did not sleep well on that first night because I was unaccustomed to rooming openly with cockroaches. I lay awake several hours, wondering what new experiences lay ahead.

The following morning I was told that I would be required to join the company union. After paying the dues and initiation fees, I received my first assignment as Junior Third Mate on board the *Atlantic*, one of the three passenger vessels operated by the company. I assumed that I would be required to wear a uniform and look squared away at all times for the passengers, a thought that did not appeal to me after four years at the academy, so I declined the assignment. I did not realize at the time that a new hire has little say in what assignment he will be given, and I would later regret my decision. I made it clear to the personnel director that I would prefer to work on a general cargo vessel. For the next several days I boarded various company vessels and observed operations, and on the fourth day I finally boarded my newly assigned ship as Junior Third Mate.

I JOIN THE *EXMINSTER*

On the morning of my fourth day in Hoboken, I walked down the street to a small coffee shop along the waterfront. As I gazed toward the piers I noticed a different ship at Pier A. She must have arrived early in the morning, because longshoremen were just opening the cargo hatches and rigging the ship's gear for discharging the cargo. This had to be the break-bulk steamship *Exminster*, to which I had been assigned. I felt apprehensive and had many questions cycling through my mind that morning. What would the crew and captain be like? Would the food be good? What hours would I be on watch, and what would be my duties? How would I learn all there was to know about the cargo gear?

I quickly finished my breakfast, headed for the main gate directly across the street, and continued on to the pier warehouse. As I began to walk into the warehouse, a forklift truck careened recklessly nearby, almost striking me head on. Many other forklifts were swiftly moving cargo in from the pier apron alongside the vessel. The warehouse was long and mostly dark, with open double doors admitting intermittent sunlight along the pier apron. The general cargo was neatly stowed on wooden pallets approximately four feet square.

Cargo was being discharged from one of the *Exminster*'s hatches while longshoremen loaded other hatches. Drafts of cargo were set upon the pier apron and quickly released from the lifting slings by longshoremen. Almost immediately a forklift was driven toward the pallet, and the operator drove the lift's two steel prongs into the space between the pallet's two wooden surfaces. The pallet was then hydraulically lifted and carried to its place of stowage inside the warehouse. Other cargo was being loaded in much the same way, except that the process was reversed. A longshoreman standing at the ship's rail would signal a fellow worker, who controlled the ship's winches, when a pallet in the lifting slings was ready to be hoisted aboard.

Cargo was handled using the "yard and stay" method, in which one boom is positioned over the hatch and the other is spotted over the dock apron. The wire falls are connected or "married" together, allowing the load to be lifted vertically from the pier, swung over the hatch, and then lowered into the hold. After the load is landed on the wooden floor, each item is stowed by several additional longshoremen. Two heavy-lift cargo booms were rigged for extra-heavy loads, such as locomotives, armored tanks, or personnel carriers. Rigging the heavy-lift boom was a task of at least four to six hours. It was necessary to remove the cargo runners from the regular winches and install heavy-lift wires to the winch drums normally utilized for the runners. I remember feeling overwhelmed by the various activities taking place simultaneously and wondering how I would ever understand it all.

The Junior Third Mate's room was small, with a sink and a mirror on the left. The bunk was opposite a varnished wooden desk. Due to the lack of air conditioning, we were supplied with a wood and canvas cot to sleep outside in hot weather. There was a common shower a short distance down the passageway. The engineers lived on the port side and the deck officers on the starboard side. The captain and radio officer had their rooms on the next deck up, with the captain's quarters always located on the starboard side. A large part of my time in my first evenings aboard was taken up with becoming familiar with the operation systems on board and discovering where everything was stowed. It was necessary to become familiar with all thirty-six crewmembers and learn their names.

While in the homeport, the ship's officers worked a day shift of eight hours, giving them evenings free to go ashore and shop or take care of last-minute matters. Each day at about noon, we walked about one block down the street from the piers to a unique restaurant and bar, which was extremely popular with the ship personnel. As I entered the front door for the first time, I was amazed to see thousands of broken clamshells strewn across the floor. In the distance was an old bar with a shining brass footrail. The establishment was divided into three sections: the bar, an average dining room, and a full-service restaurant. In those days, it was common for ship personnel to take a midday break with a few beers at lunchtime, a practice that would be grounds for termination today, due to zero tolerance requirements and the random drug and alcohol testing programs now in place. The restaurant was known as the Clam Broth House and had been popular since the turn of the century. Coming from a coastal New England town, I instantly felt comfortable in this restaurant with its seafood menu, and I don't recall ever being disappointed with a meal there.

After several days of loading, the ship was ready to be secured for sea. Each hatch opening was equipped with steel beams that fit into steel slots in the hatch perimeter. Wooden hatch boards fit tightly between the beams when the hatch was secured. These boards were three feet long and eighteen inches wide, with recessed steel handles. The main deck hatches were covered with canvas tarpaulins spread across the hatch boards. Steel battens were laid over the folded edges of the tarps. Finally, steel wedges were driven between stops welded along the sides of the hatch opening and the steel battens.

There was a great deal of learning crammed into that short time. I worked with lashing gangs and carpenter gangs engaged in securing the deck cargo for sea, and quickly learned that a break-bulk freighter was not a pretty sight after the completion of loading operations. Wooden catwalks were constructed over the deck cargo to allow shipboard personnel access from the deckhouse amidships to the bow and stern. Wire cables and turnbuckles led across the deck at various angles and in all directions. Large cargoes, such as armored personnel carriers, trucks, and bulldozers, were loaded on deck. The various types of cargo loaded in the holds were too many to list. Upon completion of loading, a final cargo plan was made up showing the location of all cargoes and their ports of discharge.

DEPARTURE, FINALLY

I remember standing at the rail outside my room, gazing at the Manhattan skyline on the night of departure and thinking, "Wow, I have really done it!" I was feeling a rush of excitement, but much apprehension, as well. Shortly after the Sandy Hook pilot disembarked in the vicinity of the Ambrose Lightship, the time came to assume my first sea watch. The captain turned toward me and said, "Ok, you have it Mr. Mate," and went below. I could not believe that I was the officer of the watch. I am certain the captain was looking out of his porthole, keeping an eye on my navigation.

My previous training had done nothing to prepare me for my relationship with the captain. Although a United States citizen, he was of Chinese descent and spoke with a slight accent. On the first day out of New York he began to do all he could to lower my self-confidence and make me feel inferior. His verbal abuse began on the day I reported aboard and continued for the next nine months. Each day the tension between us increased, until it reached a point where I began to doubt every decision I made. I could not understand what I had done to deserve this kind of treatment. When I took visual bearings on lighthouses and land objects for navigation, he tried to confuse me by voicing one number after another.

I felt that I was performing my duties well, yet he kept referring to me as a "sloth" because I worked slowly and methodically. I have always felt that accuracy and completeness are the keys to performing a job well, and that racing around only produces mistakes. He insulted and degraded me so thoroughly that I was often driven to the limits of frustration. I could not understand why he appeared to be doing his best to make my life miserable.

The first rule at sea is for the watch officer to call the captain if he has a question regarding the navigation of the vessel, but things became so bad between us that I became reluctant to call him in times of doubt, because I dreaded the abuse he was sure to give me. I considered myself very qualified to stand navigation bridge watches. The positions that I plotted were accurate and gave an adequate indication of the ship's location. On frequent occasions, the captain insisted that I obtain a fix of the vessel's position. Almost always, after he examined my work, he would utter the words, "That's Impossee-ble, that can't beee!" I will never forget the accent, which I have attempted to replicate here. Arrival watches, approaching a port of call, were especially stressful, due to his constant harassment. It is apparent to me, as I reflect upon those days, that he lacked self-confidence. Even now, after more than forty years of going to sea, arrival watches remind me of those days. Three months passed before the pieces began fitting into place, allowing me to see what was happening.

The daily abuse continued as the *Exminster* proceeded on an easterly course toward the islands of Corvo and Flores in the Azores and then toward the Strait of Gibraltar. After entering the Mediterranean Sea, the vessel called at ports in Spain, Italy, Greece, Lebanon, and Israel. The route continued through the Suez Canal and Red Sea with stops in India and Pakistan. It was then on to Hong Kong, Formosa, Vietnam, Korea, and several Japanese ports. By the time the vessel called at Yokohama, Japan, she was loaded once again and ready to proceed to San Francisco and Los Angeles. The final leg of the voyage involved calls at the Panama Canal, San Juan, Puerto Rico, and lastly, New York.

My relationship with the captain deteriorated steadily until we reached the port of Karachi, West Pakistan. One day as I was attending to my cargo-handling duties, the captain approached me and said, "Mr. Grimes, I have good news for you tonight. You're taking me out to dinner." I thought that he wanted to improve the relationship between us, which was indeed the case—but not in the way I had anticipated! The chief engineer and first assistant engineer asked where I was going when they noticed that I was putting on a coat and tie. They each grinned when I explained that I was going to dinner with the Old Man. I still did not suspect that anything was out of place. We completed our dinner and had several drinks at a plush resort hotel. Afterward, as we were returning to the ship in a taxi, the captain put his hand on my leg and began to rub my thigh. I told him in very clear language that he must remove his hand from my leg immediately. He replied, "I didn't mean to offend you."

I was so depressed and demoralized after our dinner outing that it became obvious to others on the ship. The chief engineer took me aside on one occasion and advised me to leave the ship in New York, because he feared that something would give between the captain and me. He added that he did not think it would be the captain who would break under the stress. I made it clear, however, that I would not be driven from my first assignment. As I reflect upon that exchange many years later it occurs to me that he may have been alluding to the possibility of me committing suicide. A scary thought, indeed.

One night, while working cargo in port, I called the captain on ship's business using the wheelhouse telephone. Receiving no answer, I went to the next deck and knocked on his office door. Still hearing no answer, I entered the office and knocked on the bedroom door, which I then opened with trepidation, wondering if he had passed out or, worse yet, suffered a heart attack or other serious medical event. My consternation was complete when I caught him with his hairpiece off. He threw something at me, a shoe I believe. I had not realized that he was bald and wore a false hairpiece. I am sure this incident did nothing to improve our relationship.

The captain displayed one annoying mannerism during meal

hours. Each meal, as we took our seats at the dinner table and began placing our orders, the captain would walk in with a big grin on his face and sit down at his table. He would then put both hands flat on the table in front of him with his arms out straight and utter the words, "Dee-licious, Dee-licious, Dee-licious, what tasty morsels have we today." I believe he repeated those words before every meal during two voyages around the world and a third one to India and back.

CALCUTTA

From Pakistan, the vessel proceeded on to Bombay, (now Mumbai) Cochin, Sri Lanka, Visakhapatnam, Madras, and Calcutta, all (except Sri Lanka) ports on the Indian subcontinent. Calcutta was the most depressing port that I have ever had the occasion to visit. As I made my way around the world, I made every effort to go ashore and photograph people and surroundings. Prior to going ashore in Calcutta, I was required to sign an affidavit certifying that I was an "alcoholic." Like the United States, India contains some states that are dry, with no alcohol consumption allowed. Calcutta was a dry area, and only an Indian citizen or visitor with a medical reason to consume alcohol was allowed to do so. The favored medical reason was alcoholism, so a sailor on shore leave needed a certificate stating that he was an alcoholic. I only recently learned this—on September 9, 2010, during a lightering operation in the Gulf of Mexico—from an Indian mooring master on board my vessel. All I knew 45 years ago was that if I wanted to go ashore, I needed "proof" that I was an alcoholic. The scenes that greeted me in the streets of Calcutta were like nothing I had ever witnessed ever before. Poor people lay in the street, begging, while those of the upper class stepped over them and continued on about their business. Small children by the dozens approached me with their hands out, seeking "Bakshesh," or money. I had to refuse them, because I knew that if I gave money to one, hoards of others would gather about me very soon after. One particular instance remains

as vivid in my mind today as it was on the night it happened. As I was walking along the street, returning to the ship, I looked down at an elderly Indian woman whose arms were outstretched toward me. Her eye sockets were empty, her eyes having apparently been plucked out at some time in her life. Flies were buzzing about her and crawling into and out of her sockets, while water tainted with raw sewerage trickled around her ankles. The only sounds she could utter were dull moans of pain and despair.

That cows are sacred in India quickly became apparent as I rode through the city streets in a taxicab. We had to stop frequently to allow several cows the right of way. Pedestrians, cars, and people riding bicycles added to the general confusion. A strong stench of raw sewerage and human excrement running in the gutters permeated the air. It was plain to see, as I walked through the streets, that Indian society was divided into distinct social classes. The rich went about their business, paying no attention to the poor beggars milling about the market place and alleyways.

Walking along the waterfront, I observed hundreds of large crows perched upon power lines searching for food. The people living on the cargo barges cooked their meals in the open, using dried cow dung for cooking fuel. The combustion of this fuel generated a thick smoke that rose slowly into the atmosphere, forming a brown toxic haze. Most of the cargo barges were equipped with small box-like structures that protruded from the stern over the water. Each box had a seat inside, open in the center, by means of which the people on board relieved themselves when necessary. These human wastes added to the already polluted river waters.

On board ship during cargo operations, the longshoremen worked almost around the clock with little or no sleep. They appeared thin and malnourished from lack of food and extreme working hours. During one night watch, I became extremely frustrated when I could not get the longshoremen to cooperate between the hours of midnight and eight o'clock in the morning. When I approached the chief mate with my problem, he instructed me to let them sleep, because they would be more productive during the day after getting some rest. The men sang a chant while moving huge bales of burlap sacks bundled tightly together into the wings of the hold. I would have recorded that chant, but I did not have access to a portable tape recorder at the time. Looking back, it would have been worth the trouble to buy one ashore just to have the recording.

The Hooghly River is approximately 260 miles long and connects to the Ganges River in West Bengal, India. Calcutta, a major shipping port for import and export trade, is located on this river. The port area of Calcutta is comprised of two areas where cargo ships are moored or anchored. One area is protected by locks, which remain closed when there are no ship movements. This ensures a constant water level within the port regardless of the level of the river.

At certain times of year, the Hooghly River is subject to the sudden rise in water level known as a tidal bore. This phenomenon is caused by seawater being constricted between the narrow banks of the river as it flows shoreward from the wider estuary on the coast. Such bores are often in excess of seven feet high and can approach rapidly, with little or no warning. If no berthing location is available for cargo vessels within the port limits, it is necessary to secure vessels to large mooring buoys in the river.

In such cases both port and starboard anchors, along with a shot of chain from each side, are lowered to a work float. The connecting links are disconnected at each anchor, and the two chains are laid out on the surface of the float. The standard length of a shot of chain is ninety feet, or fifteen fathoms. The work float is then towed to the stern. One shot of chain is then heaved through each of the quarter chocks so that chain remains suspended to the water from each quarter. A work crew then secures one end on the ship and the other end to a large mooring buoy in the river. One shot of chain is then lowered from each bow to a mooring buoy ahead of the ship. The chains are secured so that they lead across the bow and stern from starboard to port and from port to starboard. The ship's crew all hoped for a berth within the precincts of the port in order to avoid working the entire day to moor the ship. I was looking forward to experiencing a tidal bore, but none occurred while we were there.

Upon the completion of cargo operations, a large amount of wood, or dunnage, was left strewn across the decks. This wood had been used to provide void spaces between the cargo and the hull of the ship. Usually it was contaminated and could not be re-used, so it was disposed of by means of a system that benefited the villagers as well as the vessel. As the ship proceeded downriver to the sea, the dunnage was tossed into the water. Small boats standing by along the riverbanks quickly rowed out and salvaged the wood planks. The villagers gained wood for fires or construction needs, and the ship disposed of waste wood with no cost and little effort.

After leaving India, the *Exminster* proceeded through the Strait of Sumatra and on to Hong Kong. Hong Kong was built on the slopes of large hills, with very little dock space available for ships. Most cargo vessels were forced to anchor or moor to buoys in the harbor for cargo operations. Cargo of all kinds was transported to the ships on board small, motor-powered craft. These boats were usually constructed of wood and beautifully varnished, with potted plants on deck. It was apparent that the boats were actually the homes of entire families. On one occasion I observed three generations at work. It was necessary to take a launch to shore if we wanted to do

any shopping. Ashore, I was measured for two sport jackets and purchased a beautiful, ornate, hand-carved wooden chest. It was incredible to look on as two workers carried that heavy chest up the steep gangway the next day. I also purchased a new Plath sextant that day, which I carried with me on every voyage for seven years.

After calling at Hong Kong, the vessel proceeded on to two ports in Nationalist China, or Formosa (now Taiwan), where cargo was discharged and more was loaded for the United States, and then, finally, it was on to Vietnam. A significant quantity of military cargo destined for the war effort there was stowed in the lower holds. At each calling port on our round-the-world voyage, cargo loaded on the U.S. East Coast had been discharged from each hatch while cargo bound for the United States was simultaneously loaded. This operation often required shifting cargo to prevent overstowing the existing cargo. Ten thousand tons of toilet bowls and some commercial cargo had been loaded in Genoa, Italy, for Vietnam.

Due to a logistical bottleneck caused by the influx of huge

quantities of cargo to the port of Saigon, many commercial ships were anchored at the mouth of the Saigon River upon our arrival. The captain was sure that the *Exminster* would transit the river with minimal delay because we were an American-flagged vessel carrying military cargo. Part of his premise was true, as the vessel was called into port within several days to discharge its military cargo. Upon completion of this operation, however, we received orders to anchor at the mouth of the Saigon River until summoned for the remainder of the discharge. Each morning the pilot vessel came toward the anchored ships, and one vessel proceeded into the river. At about sunset, one more vessel transited the river. We were anchored at the mouth of the river for a total of thirty days.

During this period I had the welcome opportunity to ride in a launch to shore for a little break from the monotony of the daily eight-hour anchor watch. While ashore, I met an American soldier who suggested that we go to a bar he frequented. I climbed on a motorcycle with him, and we proceeded down a long, winding road. The bar was in a village deep in the jungle, which made me somewhat apprehensive. While enjoying a few beers, I heard several soldiers discussing the location of the bar and noting that Viet Cong were nearby, which made me even more nervous. When I expressed concern for our safety, one soldier said, "Don't worry, the only way out of here is the way we came in. The Viet cong is in control of the rest of the area." We returned to the ship safely, for which I was thankful. I believe the soldiers were putting me on, knowing that I was a merchant seaman. There was some animosity between the soldiers and the merchant marine because of the difference in the pay. I was receiving double pay for being on a ship traversing waters in a war zone, plus an additional fifteen percent bonus for having ammunition on board. I felt guilty receiving these bonuses, given that our soldiers were risking their lives for relatively low salaries.

From Vietnam, our round-the-world odyssey took us to Inchon and Pusan in Korea. Inchon was definitely the coldest port that I have ever visited. The vessel was moored close to a breakwater during cargo operations, and I was stationed at the stern to watch

for signs of the anchor dragging. As I stood my watch that night, feeling cold right to the bone, my thoughts turned to the soldiers who had fought in the Korean conflict, and of how they must have suffered during the invasion of Inchon.

The final foreign ports were Kobe, Shimizu, Nagoya, and Yokohama in Japan. After what seemed like an eternity, we returned to United States soil as the ship pulled into San Francisco. After several days there, we moved on to Los Angeles. One incident remains clearly in mind regarding handling special cargo while the vessel was docked in Los Angeles. Special cargo lockers were used for stowage of cargoes that were highly susceptible to pilferage due to longshoremen. While I was checking out cases of radios in Los Angeles, the checker and I agreed on the number of cases discharged and then broke for lunch. When the checker returned, he informed me that the shore tally had come up one case short. I knew something was amiss and that I was in trouble, because I had failed to obtain the checker's signature before breaking for lunch. During the afternoon, I noticed that each of the longshoremen was listening to the World Series on his own radio.

I informed the chief officer, who became extremely upset upon hearing the report. Shortly after the vessel sailed, he discovered the torn remains of a case of radios in one of the mast houses. He and I then discussed a plan to disguise the loss of the radios. I reported that I had noticed cargo being handled roughly during the day and that several cases had been caught in the cargo nets after falling from the cargo slings. We composed a letter and forwarded it to the company office, stating that it was our feeling that the missing case had been lost overboard due to mishandling by the longshoremen. The company mail arrived on board when we put in at San Juan, Puerto Rico. Upon inspection, the mail revealed that the office personnel believed the story and I was off the hook.

Often the special cargo locker was used for the stowage of wine and hard liquor. The chief mate made it a policy to offer one case of liquor to the longshoreman gang foreman at the beginning of the day. If this was not done there was a good chance that one or two bottles would be ripped from each of several cartons. Rather than have a cargo damage claim arising out of the loss of one bottle from a number of cases, it was less troublesome and more economical for the ship to account for the loss of one complete case.

While discharging in New York, I noticed a longshoreman in the cargo hatch putting on a number or shirts and pants while discharging clothing that had been loaded in Hong Kong. He then put on work coveralls that were many sizes too big for his body size. I decided that I was going to call this person on the fact that I had observed him stealing the cargo. As the men were going down the gangway for lunch, I stopped him and informed him that I wanted him to accompany me to the chief mate's office. He had a cargo hook in his hand, which he promptly held in front of my face. As he did so, he said, "Mr. Mate, I am going down that gangway and if you have any other ideas I will put this cargo hook in your face." I doubt that he was serious about his intentions, however I was not in a position to question them. I wished him a good day and told him to enjoy his lunch. I was not going to be a hero for the sake of some pants and shirts.

THE PANAMA CANAL

Our passage to San Juan included a transit across the Isthmus of Panama via the Panama Canal. Much has been written and said about the amazing feat of engineering called the Panama Canal, but until it is experienced firsthand, the true magnitude of the accomplishment cannot be realized. The idea of building a canal across the Isthmus of Panama had been considered as far back as the sixteenth century. The French attempted it beginning in 1880, but failed. In 1914, after experiencing 5,600 deaths from malaria and other causes, the United States finally succeeded in opening a way for marine traffic to make voyages between the Pacific Ocean and the Atlantic Ocean without rounding Cape Horn. This was a major breakthrough, given the huge amount of time saved by eliminating the need for vessels to voyage around the Horn at the southern tip of South America.

Engineers were aware that a large amount of excavation would be necessary no matter what method was chosen to construct the canal. The final design consisted of a series of locks that would allow a vessel to be raised by stages to a predetermined level and later lowered back to sea level. A lake was formed by the construction of dams to trap the heavy tropical rainfall. In order to cross the higher mountain peaks in the middle portion of the isthmus, it was necessary to cut through them using heavy excavation equipment and thousand of hours of labor. This "cut" is known as the Galliard Cut.

The lock system raises ships 85 feet to the level of Gatun Lake. After vessels have transited through the Galliard Cut and Gatun Lake, another set of locks lowers them back to sea level. There are two locks on the Pacific side, one pair of chambers at Miraflores and one chamber at Pedro Miguel. On the Atlantic side there is one set of three chambers at Gatun. Each lock chamber has an approach wall extending out from the lock, which allows canal seamen to row out to an approaching ship and pass rope messengers to the deck crew. Heaving on the two messengers— one on each side of the vessel—hauls aboard a wire cable from each side of the lock, by means of which the ship is connected to specially designed rail vehicles, called "mules," on the lock walls. Once the ship is positioned inside the lock chamber, gates close behind and the water level rises or falls. The raising or lowering is accomplished by means of gravity using water from man-made Gatun Lake. Tropical rainfall replenishes the water used by the lock system.

Experiencing a canal transit is the high point of any voyage from one coast to the other. The rate at which the water level is changed by gravity within each lock is surprising. During the canal passage, canal seamen bring local goods on board to sell to ship personnel. This is a welcome opportunity to buy locally made products without having to go ashore to shop. Ship personnel usually have no opportunity to go ashore in the Canal Zone unless the vessel has anchored or docked for fuel or cargo operations.

Finally, after four and a half months, I stood at the rail and gazed at the Statue of Liberty and the Manhattan skyline once again. I would soon return home for ten days of vacation before setting out once again on a three-month trip to India and back. In all, nine months would pass before I would finally get out from under the miserable treatment of the abusive captain.

But my inaugural round-the-world voyage had given me an ideal opportunity to observe other cultures and lifestyles. I took hundreds of photographs, most of which remain in my collection today. I'd seen places that remain vivid in my memory today, including the Strait of Messina in Italy, Hong Kong, the Sumatra Straits, and Japan's Inland Sea. These areas stand out because of the high density of vessel traffic and beautiful scenery.

The *Exminster* (shown on the cover) had been designed and built by the United States Maritime Administration in 1943. Her hull was constructed of heavy overlapping steel plates riveted together. Her bow, or stem, was nearly vertical, and her stern curved gracefully, with her rudderpost clearly visible above the waterline. Her profile and classic old lines were appealing to the eye. She had seven cargo hatches, with four located forward of the deck superstructure and three located aft. The number four hold was accessed through two smaller hatches, one on each side. Special cargo lockers—used for the stowage of liquor and beer as well as cigarettes—were fitted in the upper and lower tweendecks of the number four hold. Even though there were locks on the doors of these lockers, longshoremen still found ways to steal this coveted and portable cargo. They were masters at pilfering cargo right out from under our eyes.

Specialized bulk cargo tanks were fitted in number four lower hold. These tanks were used for the stowage of bulk liquid cargoes such as tallow and cashew nut shell oil. Any skin contact with the latter could cause a severe rash. The irritation and pain of the rash I experienced after going to the head with the oil on my hands remains clear and immediate in my memory. Such things are less likely today, because industry regulations now require that all oils or bulk liquids loaded on board a ship must be accompanied by a material safety data sheet, or MSDS, listing all the possible hazards that may be encountered by handlers.

Several holds were fitted with lockers capable of maintaining temperatures appropriate for refrigerated cargo. Numbers one, four, and seven hatches were equipped with two cargo booms, while the remaining hatches had four booms each. The wheelhouse or bridge was small compared with those on ships today. A large wooden steering wheel and hydraulic telemotor were centrally mounted on a pedestal amidships. The hydraulic system always leaked, which caused a slow drip from a valve under the steering wheel. It was necessary to empty the small can that was slung under the valve at frequent intervals. To the right of the wooden steering wheel stood a gray metal stand with a handle at the top. This housed the electric steering control mechanism and gyrocompass repeater. Two radar units were located alongside the steering pedestals. Radar had been developed during World War II, and many older captains were reluctant to allow ship personnel to use radar in clear weather, fearing excessive wear in the radar units. They did not realize that radars perform best when supplied with power all the time. Today's ships have radars either operating or on standby at all times when underway. A radio direction finder, or RDF, of questionable accuracy and a magnetic compass completed the inventory of navigation equipment.

Although each ship was equipped with a sextant for the officers' use, most mates carried their own so they could be confident of the instrument's accuracy. The *Exminster*'s bos'n (boatswain, in landsman language) was having difficulty understanding the principles of celestial navigation, so he approached me with a proposition. He and I agreed that for each hour I helped him understand navigation, he would teach me deck seamanship for an equal amount of time. This arrangement resulted in his receiving a Second Mate License and me receiving much needed practical deck knowledge. Most of the shipboard navigation was celestial, and it was surprisingly accurate. I used my new Plath sextant on watch each day and often took stars with the second mate, who was the ship's navigation officer. Our positions agreed very closely most of the time. One evening, I noticed that we differed only by two miles. He said it was too bad that I was that far off. When I asked why it was me that was off, he replied, "Because you are the third mate and I am the second mate."

EXTRA DUTIES AT SEA

The third mate was required to perform extra duties at sea, such as drawing the daily weather map, maintaining the inventory of flags, keeping the smooth log, and maintaining the ship's firefighting and lifesaving equipment. In addition to those mentioned above, there were chart corrections and Notices to Mariners to bring up to date, a duty I shared with the other mates on board. These duties were always performed while off watch.

Each ship cooperated in a government operated weather program in which vessels transmitted coded weather messages to a shore station. These messages were then analyzed and compiled into a periodic radio transmission back to the ships. This weather message, received daily by the radio officer and delivered to my room, consisted of about twenty coded groups of five numbers. When properly decoded with the aid of the weather report manual, it enabled me to draw up a comprehensive weather map that included all symbols and notations. Today, ships are equipped with electronic means of receiving and printing prepared weather information. I enjoyed decoding these messages and preparing the map each day. It was a diversion from the monotonous daily routine. The officers on watch made regular entries into the rough log when at sea and during cargo watch. The third mate was required to copy all of the entries in ink into a smooth logbook. It was up to him as to how and when this duty was performed. I sometimes did it every two or three days, but on occasion I let it go for a week or two and could never seem to catch up. It is a wonder that I did not develop carpal tunnel syndrome from all that writing.

The vessel maintained an extensive flag inventory, which covered all of the countries to be visited on the projected route. Proper flag etiquette requires visiting vessels to fly the flag of the host country at the foremast head, and its national flag at the stern. The shipping company would be subjected to a hefty fine levied by the host government if this courtesy was not extended. Often there was only one flag on hand, which was usually torn and tattered to the point that it was necessary to hem the edges by hand in order to make it presentable. Although I had little sewing expertise, I had to learn those skills rather quickly.

The lifeboat equipment was checked periodically and out-of-date supplies were replaced when necessary. Items, such as signal flares, water, and food were dated and good for a specified number of years. One day during one of these inventories, I opened one of the food packets to taste it out of curiosity. It was not bad, and I'm sure it would have tasted really good if our lives had depended upon it.

The lifeboats were regularly inspected for evidence of deterioration or corrosion in the hull. I once accompanied a United States Coast Guard inspector as he examined the hull of one of our lifeboats. He was equipped with a deadly looking pointed chipping hammer, with which he tested spots on the hull that were in questionable condition. I watched in amazement as he knocked six holes in one of our boats. He told me later that it was not unusual to find this. He went on to explain that the presence of paint bubbles, even if no rust is visible, suggests that corrosion has been taking place under the paint, resulting in hull deterioration.

All of the firefighting equipment was required to be inventoried and checked at periodic intervals. The dates indicating when the equipment in question had last been tested were checked and updated. Fire stations and fire extinguishers had to be stenciled and painted frequently. I usually did this on my off-watch hours at sea.

I thought that the "Adopt a Ship Program" was the most rewarding and enjoyable extra assignment. The company participated in a program with schools across the country, which enabled the students to correspond with the ship's officers. Each ship was assigned to one school from a randomly chosen location. The ship's agent delivered a packet containing the students' letters to the ship every few months. The captain assigned each of the officers several letters to answer. I enjoyed answering the letters, taking one question at a time. The questions covered all aspects of life on board ship, such as when we worked, what we ate, and what it was like to be away from home and our family. It was a welcome break from the monotonous daily routine of long sea passages.

A few weeks ago I did some research regarding the fate of the *Exminster*. I was curious as to what the company had done with the vessel since I had last served on board. I learned that it had been delivered to the scrap yard to be disassembled in 1972. One interesting fact, resulting from the research pertained to an elementary school in a small town in the state of Washington. One of the teachers had written to the company with a request for a piece of equipment, which could serve as a remembrance of the school's association with the ship and its personnel. The company salvaged the ship's large brass bell with the name of the vessel and the date of construction engraved on its surface. It was later shipped to the school and is now displayed in a prominent location on school grounds. If I ever travel to the west coast I may visit the school and stand by the bell, as I ponder my time spent, both good and bad while serving on board *Exminster*.

NAVIGATION ROUTINE

The term "day's work" refers to the 24-hour period from noon to noon on board ship. The vessel's position is noted at noon by means of a specific process known as the latitude at noon sight. The navigator watches the sun when it bears due north or south, at which time the sun's altitude is recorded. The ship's precise latitude is then calculated using tables of astronomical data. Several lines of position of the sun are taken during the afternoon. In the evening the second mate calculates the most opportune time to observe the stars based upon the vessel's estimated position and previously taken sun lines. There should be enough daylight to see the horizon clearly, and enough darkness to view the chosen stars through the high-powered telescope mounted on the sextant. Three or more stars are observed, weather permitting. The angle between the stars should be close to 45 degrees for the most accurate fix.

The navigator then works out the figures and plots the lines of position on a plotting sheet. These lines should cross at one point under ideal conditions. This rarely happens, however, due to observer error, weather conditions and the movement of the ship. Most often, a small triangle is formed and the vessel's position is estimated based upon that triangle. The vessel's track is plotted from this position during the night, based upon estimated course, speed, current, and wind information. This process is known as "dead reckoning," a contraction of the term "deduced reckoning." The dead reckoning plot is carried forward until morning star time, when the second mate takes star sights once again and plots the resulting ship's position. The third mate obtains several lines of position using the sun between 0800 and the point in time when the sun bears due north or south of the vessel. Using this information he maintains a running position until it is possible to obtain the noon position by crossing the noon latitude line with the morning sun lines. The process has now been completed over a period of 24 hours, hence the term "day's work."

At least once a watch, observations are made of the sun or stars, as the case may be, using a bearing device mounted over a gyrocompass repeater. A bearing is taken and compared with the bearing calculated using Greenwich Mean Time and the vessel's known position. The difference between these bearings represents the compass error. This error and all headings are noted in the vessel logbook. It is important to maintain a record of compass error in case a loss of power should make the gyrocompass inoperable and necessitate the use of the ship's magnetic compass instead.

When underway at sea, it is essential for the mate on watch to keep an alert lookout at all times. At sea, the deckhand is often chipping rust or painting in the area of the wheelhouse and cannot be depended upon to keep a good lookout, so it is up to the watch officer to be aware of any oncoming vessel traffic. It is easy to be distracted when attempting to make chart corrections or update navigation publications in the chartroom. The watch officer may think that he or she can work on chart corrections and still remember to check for oncoming ship traffic, but I found this not to be the case. One sunny day in the Pacific Ocean, while working in the chartroom, I felt a strong sensation that something was amiss and that I should go to the wheelhouse and check the situation. Fortunately for me, I checked, because a ship was approaching six miles away dead ahead on a reciprocal course to ours. I took action to avoid collision, but I learned a good lesson—to limit my future chart correcting to times when the vessel was at anchor or docked.

PROFESSIONAL TRAINING

As in all other professions, it is necessary for personnel to undergo regular training. In recent years, additional requirements have been added to those already in place, which are monitored by the United States Coast Guard. In addition to a professional license as a merchant marine officer, it is now necessary to hold a certificate of Standards of Training, Certification and Watchkeeping. (STCW) Mariners are also required to hold a Transport Workers Identification Certificate. (TWIC) In order to obtain a TWIC card, one must pass an extensive background check. This is a result of new and more stringent standards put in place due to the threat of terrorism in recent years.

Deck officers must pass a course in basic safety training, and bridge resource management, among others. The most challenging of these training requirements is the firefighting training. Over the years I have attended many firefighting schools, which have benefitted me a great deal. I think the primary value of this type of "hands-on" training is that the student is given the opportunity to actually put the fires out while working in teams with others in the class. Students are required to don a breathing apparatus and enter smoke-filled spaces where there is little or no visibility. A maze (complex series of tunnels where it is easy to get lost) is used to help the student learn to proceed by feeling areas around them, not only from side to side but above and below. Fires in interior spaces are extinguished, as well as in the field during these courses.

Mariners are given the confidence that, should they encounter a similar situation in real life on board a ship, they will be able to act in a positive and effective manner. In order to be effective and prevent personal injury, it is essential that all students work together with the common goal of combating and extinguishing the fire while watching out for one another's safety.

During my career I have experienced several instances, which are examples of what can happen if each team does not do their part in the exercise, or if the instructors do not follow due diligence while monitoring the training program. On one occasion my team had already passed through the smoke house with each member wearing a breathing apparatus. When the team reached the roof of the building the instructor informed us that we would be returning the way we had come to the ground. The only difference was that we would not be wearing the breathing apparatus. We had been taught to feel the area around us and to stay low while breathing as little as possible. I was last in the group when I reached the exit hatch. It was a total shock when the hatch was suddenly slammed shut in my face while someone began tightening the dogs (latches) on the steel hatch. I tend to be negatively affected by claustrophobia in tight spaces. As soon as the door was closed I began to bang on it as hard as I could to draw attention. One of the instructors took the dogs off and opened the door to find me in a very upset state. All of the others got a big laugh when the instructor said, "Oh, I guess we forgot somebody!" I failed to see the humor and vowed to bring this to the attention of the school administration when the time was right.

On another occasion I was placed in the nozzle position with the team instructor next to me. It was the duty of the team to move in on the fire with a solid stream of water aimed at the fire. The team next to us was to provide a cooling shield of water so that we could advance closer to the flames and extinguish the fire. I was wearing proper protective clothing, including rubber boots, gloves, firemen's suit, helmet and goggles. As my team advanced toward the flames, the heat grew very intense and I wondered why the cooling shield was not there. I felt the skin of my left leg under the rubber boot beginning to burn, as well as a portion of my left arm. There was a gap between the suit and the cuff of my left glove. I told the instructor that something was amiss and that I was getting physically harmed.

He pushed me toward the fire and yelled, "Lets go get it!" I stated that I would drop the nozzle and back away from the heat unless he gave the order for all of the teams to withdraw to a safer area. He did so and the fire was extinguished by means of a fixed system. The next day I showed my burns to the instructor. He laughed and said that he thought that the fire was hot enough. After arriving home I went to my family physician for treatment. I am not usually the kind of person to make a big deal of things like this, however I felt that this had gone a little too far. I composed a letter to the school administration describing the two experiences and made suggestions as to how this could be avoided in the future. I told a friend who was scheduled to attend the same school a month later. Upon his return to Rockport, he said that my letter must have done some good because they went out of their way to emphasize the possibility of personal injury.

～ WEEKLY DRILLS ～

Fire and abandon-ship drills were required to be held at least once each week. The fire drill was usually held first on most ships, which is not a good practice. The drills should be varied so that the crew does not grow complacent and too accustomed to the same routine each time. On one occasion after a new captain reported on board, the abandon-ship signal was sounded and a good portion of the crew proceeded to their fire stations. The captain said that he varied the order of the drills on every ship when he first went aboard, often catching the crew in similar fashion.

One of my favorite drills was the line-throwing drill, which was held every three months. The cannon used to fire the heavy metal projectile to which the line was attached was called a Lyle Gun, named after Commander David A. Lyle, who invented it in 1877. Although ours was somewhat smaller than the original design, it was extremely effective. Lyle designed the device for use by the United States Lifesaving Service in saving the lives of seamen in distress in the days of sailing ships. We loaded ours with a half charge of powder and paper wadding prior to firing it. The principle of its operation had not changed since the lifesaving days; only the size and scope of the equipment had changed for shipboard use. Today, ships are equipped with self -propelled rocked devices and flares for emergency use.

THE *SIR JOHN FRANKLIN*

My next assignment was as third mate aboard a C-1 class ship named the *Sir John Franklin*. This class of vessel had five cargo hatches, three forward and two aft of the superstructure amidships. My new captain was a short, stocky fellow, who was extremely fond of cigars. Most any time of day he could be seen standing on the bridge wing, intently inhaling and exhaling the smoke of his pungent cigars. *Sir John Franklin* had been chartered by the United States military to supply weapons and materiel for the war effort in Vietnam. I joined the vessel in Bayonne, New Jersey, ready to begin another nine-month tour of duty. I fully anticipated and received a much less stressful tour this time around.

Sir John Franklin sailed from New York Harbor to the Strait of Gibraltar, through the Mediterranean Sea and the Suez Canal, and then on to Vietnam via the Sumatra Straits. Contrary to the voyage of the *Exminster,* this voyage was solely intended to transport military cargo. The vessel called at Cam Ranh Bay, Nha Trang, and Saigon in Vietnam, with an occasional trip to the Philippine Islands. On one occasion we carried damaged military vehicles from Vietnam to the Philippines, where the remains were to be stripped for spare parts. As they were lowered into the hatches, I wondered how many servicemen had been killed or wounded inside each. While anchored in Cam Ranh Bay, we discharged rocket ammunition to amphibious craft alongside. These craft loaded up to four pallets per trip and transported them to the beach for discharge ashore.

Once, while discharging to one of these craft, a pallet slipped out of the lifting cables and sank to the bottom of the bay. The military representative informed us that it would not be a problem due to inefficiency and lack of supervision on the beach.

Once, while anchored in Nha Trang Harbor, United States Navy gunboats began circling the ship, dropping concussion grenades set to explode underwater in case enemy divers were planting explosives on our hull. A ship had been blown up a week before in that exact location. Each time one of these grenades detonated, it sounded like a huge hammer hitting the side of the vessel, according to the engineers. As we transited the Saigon River on one trip, I was on the wing of the bridge taking pictures when the Vietnamese pilot rushed out to the bridge wing, saying emphatically, "You get inside, they shoot you." Snipers had shot at several vessels just a few weeks prior to our arrival at the mouth of the river.

One day, several shipmates and I took a launch to shore to explore a Vietnamese village near the base. Because the village was off limits to merchant seamen, we planned to sneak over the sand dunes to avoid being detected by the military guards patrolling the road. We made it over the dunes, but as we were making our way toward the village, I heard a click and looked up to see the barrel of a rifle pointed at me. A United States Marine guard told us to return to the ship immediately. We began walking down the road, but he made us go back up over the dunes the same way we had come, just to give us a hard time.

Upon completing its discharge of cargo, the ship proceeded to San Francisco and Los Angeles to load more military cargo, for the return voyage to Vietnam. Following discharge of the West Coast cargo, we made our way back to New York Harbor via the Suez Canal and the Mediterranean.

As we approached the canal in ballast, the 1967 Arab-Israeli War was escalating. Anticipating the closure of the canal, our captain decided to heave to while awaiting receipt of a diversion message. The expected message was indeed received, but not before the radio officer had made several attempts to request orders and had informed the master that atmospheric conditions were poor and the chances of a message getting through were questionable. The captain insisted that he would log the radio officer for "Direct disobedience to a lawful command at sea." He went through with the logging, causing the radio officer to lose three days' pay. Several months later, the radio officer contacted me at home and asked if I would give a deposition upholding his position so that he could clear his record. The case was resolved, and "Sparks" had his pay returned and his record cleared.

SHIPS PASSING IN THE NIGHT

At night on long ocean voyages I enjoyed signaling to passing ships, using the signal light on the bridge wing to break the monotony of the watch. This involved removing the canvas cover from the light and standing out in the weather. After sending the general call sign to a passing ship, I would wait until the other vessel acknowledged, then I'd request the vessel's name and destination. On one occasion, much to my surprise, it was another American Export-Isbrandtsen Lines vessel. I asked whether anyone on board had graduated from Maine Maritime Academy, and received an affirmative reply. I then learned that the person I was signaling was a classmate and friend from Rockport. It amazed me that two vessels meeting and passing one another three miles apart in that great expanse of ocean could have two close friends aboard.

Communication between the shore signal tower and the ship upon arrival in port was achieved by means of the Morse signal light. This was before the time of VHF radios. The officers aboard the ships, to which I was assigned, were generally not proficient at Morse code so they would call me to the bridge to fill that void. This was an excellent way to earn some overtime pay. I thought of how fortunate I was to have had such excellent training in the sea scouts.

About half way through the 12 to 4 watch on a calm tropical night in the Pacific Ocean an incident occurred, which will always remain etched in my mind. While standing on the port bridge wing enjoying my coffee and looking at the stars, I noticed the running lights of an approaching vessel on a reciprocal course to ours. After running a plot of the vessel's track on the radar and determining the closest point of approach, I concluded that she would pass on my port side about one mile away at the closest point. I was looking at the two white range lights one higher than the other. The lowest one was to the left, which agreed with my radar plot. I also observed the red sidelight, indicating a routine port to port passing. In a situation such as this I always kept a close eye on the other vessel until she had passed.

When the other vessel drew within 1 to 2 miles on my port bow, the two white lights suddenly began to line up. At the same time, I saw the green sidelight come into view. The adrenalin began flowing at that point, as I realized that a serious collision situation was rapidly developing. The helmsman was already steering by hand because it was the policy of the master to use hand steering in all close quarters situations. I ordered the helmsman to put the wheel hard right and was about to ring the general alarm when I noticed that the other vessel's white range lights began to open and the red light came back into my view. I know that both vessels passed at a safe distance, but it seemed as if I could have thrown a baseball on the other vessel's deck! I will never know why the other ship suddenly came left and began to cross my bow. Perhaps it was a mechanical problem with the steering or faulty communication between the other ship's watch officer and helmsman. Whatever the reason, the end result was favorable.

As mentioned above, there were no VHF radios on the bridge at that time to enable vessels to communicate with one another. Today, ships are equipped with VHF radios, AIS (Automated Information System) computer plotting and tracking devices, and ultra modern radar plotting aids. That situation could have been averted at a point where both vessels would have had more than ample opportunity to identify one another by voice communication. Both vessels would then have come to an agreement and passed on the necessary information early enough to avoid a close quarters situation. Under normal circumstances a meeting situation, such as the one described above occurred frequently. I have passed hundreds of ships without incident, but this was one time that I will never forget.

FLYING CLOUD

Home for my next tour at sea was to be the *Flying Cloud*, a C-2 class vessel with the same hatch configuration as the *Sir John Franklin* but with some differences in cargo handling gear and general profile. The captain was a distinguished man who always dressed in a clean khaki uniform, complete with tie and officer's cap. He was extremely particular regarding proper flag etiquette and several other details. Knowing what I know now regarding obsessive-compulsive disorder, I would say that he fit that profile. He required that shore watchmen be stationed about the ship in port to provide added security. Each morning, a watchman was on standby at the foremast, holding the flag of the host nation, while another was stationed on the stern with the American flag. The mate on watch was ready on the bridge with a whistle and the company house flag. At 0800, as the clock struck eight bells, the mate on the bridge blew the whistle, and all three flags were raised simultaneously.

The chief mate was constantly frustrated by this routine, because it took valuable labor away from ongoing cargo operations. The captain's obsessive behavior was apparent in other ways as well. He insisted that the ship's bell be rung every half hour with the proper number of strikes. If he did not hear the sound of the bell, whether in port or at sea, he called the bridge or cargo watch officer, demanding to know why. Some of us took particular notice of the number of crackers he consumed at afternoon teatime. He always ate three soda crackers and drank a single cup of tea without fail.

Satellite television and video machines were not available on board in those days, so reading was our daily pastime. Not having any books in my room, I searched the small ship's library and found a book entitled *Atlas Shrugged*, by Ayn Rand. One afternoon, as I was sitting on deck reading, the captain happened along and said, "Oh, I see you are reading Ayn Rand. We will have to have daily discussions on it." I was having a great deal of difficulty understanding what the book was about, so the discussions did not last long. We tried it a few times, but I lost interest and did not carry through.

As the ship was departing port one beautiful summer day, the mess boy burst into the wheelhouse screaming that the second cook was going to knife the baker! The captain calmly turned toward me with his hands clasped behind his back and said, "Mr. Grimes, will you please take care of this matter?" I was shocked to realize that I was in a potentially life-threatening situation, but I followed orders, and after considerable negotiation was able to take possession of the knife. Several crewmembers and I confined the second cook to his room. Upon returning to the bridge, I informed the captain that the situation had been successfully diffused and that I had left the knife in his quarters. His reaction was as though it was all in a day's work, but I had been a nervous wreck throughout the entire experience.

Daily ship maintenance and overhaul of the cargo gear was essential. The accumulation of rust on the decks of all merchant ships was a constant maintenance headache, especially in tropical climates. "Fish oil" (a mixture of several substances) was rolled on the decks periodically with long-handled rollers and left to dry in the hot sun for approximately one month. The deck crew then scraped the loose rust sheets from the deck with long-handled ice scrapers. The process was repeated on a regular schedule and proved extremely effective. "Slushing" the cargo runners was a daily routine for the deck hands. A black, oily substance was applied by hand, using a rag. It was often necessary for the person performing this duty to be suspended from a wooden Bos'n chair.

THE *EXPORTER*

The *Exporter,* which made voyages to the Mediterranean with stops at Iskenderun and Izmir, in Turkey was a sister ship to the *Exminster*. After taking a well-deserved summer vacation, I reported on board and prepared to sail east once again across the Atlantic Ocean. The main cargo to be transported from Turkey was tobacco, which was shipped in two basic forms, leaf and scrap. Leaf is used for the manufacture of cigars and is treated as a valuable cargo. Scrap is used in the manufacture of cigarettes. No part of the bale could be allowed to contact any surfaces in the hold. In order to prevent this from happening, a responsible crewmember was stationed in the hatch where the tobacco was being loaded. First, a layer of boards, or dunnage, was laid over the floor of the hatch, followed by another layer placed at a ninety-degree angle. Sheets of clean plywood were then laid over the dunnage, followed by sheets of corrugated paper. This provided a clean surface on which to stow the bales. The bales were further prevented from coming into contact with any part of the sides of the hold by wrapping, taping, and stapling the sweat battens and all metal stanchions with corrugated paper. Sweat battens are permanently fixed strips of wood lining the sides of a hold, and they could have been tainted by contact with previous cargo.

It was challenging work, supervising the stowage of bales while ensuring that paper was fastened where needed. Few, if any, of the men working in the hold spoke English, adding to the challenge. Once, while at work in the lower hold, a longshoreman grabbed the staple gun and began shooting his buddies with staples. I was able to wrest the gun from him after ducking several staples. After many such trips, almost no cargo was damaged, a testament to our efficient stowage process.

The ship called at Boston twice, but the longshoremen there were so difficult to work with that the company began shipping most of the cargo destined for Boston overland from New York. Boston longshoremen would simply walk off the ship and refuse to work at the slightest provocation, costing the company much lost time.

GENERAL CARGO FACTS

Below are listed some of the more unusual facts regarding the cargo that I carried during the time that I served on board the break-bulk freighters.

Shark Fins are loaded in burlap bags and require stowage on deck, far from other cargoes. Shark fin soup is a Japanese delicacy.

Magnesium is highly reactive and will ignite in contact with water. Once, after stowing bags of magnesium ore on deck, it began to rain, causing the bags to begin smoldering.

Leaf Tobacco is shipped in bales and is used for manufacturing cigars. It is highly subject to damage when it comes in contact with contaminated surfaces.

Scrap Tobacco is shipped in bales and is used for manufacturing cigarettes. It, too, is highly susceptible to damage when it comes in contact with contaminated surfaces.

Cashew Nut Shell Oil causes a rash if it contacts human skin. I experienced the burning, painful sensation once after getting it on my hands and body.

Cashew Nuts are shipped in gallon cans, packed two to a pack.

They are crated using wooden strapping.

EXPORT BUILDER AND EXPORT BUYER

In 1970 the maritime industry was beginning its transition to the intermodal age of cargo transportation between land and sea. Ships were retrofitted so that 20- and 40-foot-long containers could be efficiently loaded and transported. Specialized ships were being designed and built, which could carry the maximum number of containers. In the intermodal system of transportation, cargo is loaded into a container and then shipped by rail or truck to the pier. It can then be loaded aboard the ship and later discharged and transported to the final point of destination without exposing the cargo inside to pilferage or damage.

The *Export Builder* and *Export Buyer* were to be my new homes at sea for the next two years. Designed as break-bulk freighters, they had been modified during construction in order to accommodate the maximum number of containers. Corner fittings or sockets were welded to the deck on each side of the hatches and on top of each hatch. These sockets matched the location of the container corners. The lower holds could not be altered from the original hull design, however. Due to the curvature of the hulls, it was necessary to rig snatch blocks and use cargo runners to pull the containers toward the skin of the ships for stowage in their lower holds. After each container was in place, it was lashed with wire and turnbuckles and shored with lumber where necessary. This was a time-consuming and labor-intensive operation, which delayed sailings considerably. (Today, ships are fitted with dedicated cells that allow each container to slide along a vertical track, and the containers are stacked one over another, minimizing handling delays.) These ships followed a round-trip route from New York through the Panama Canal to the Far East.

The cargo hatches were hydraulically operated with a hand-operated remote-control lever. They consisted of multiple sections, four on the main deck and three in each tweendeck. The mate on watch was required to operate the hatch covers while working cargo in port. This kept me constantly in motion for entire eight-hour watches as I attempted to stay one step ahead of the longshoremen. In the tweendecks, two sections nearest the bulkheads were operated initially, with the third operated by activating a separate control. The first two sections rarely opened all the way, making it necessary to connect two wire pendants attached to turnbuckles with pad eyes welded to the bulkhead. After opening the two leafs as far as possible, the pendants were hooked into eyes on the cover. The cover was forced open by twisting turnbuckles, thereby allowing a fitting to engage that would allow the hydraulic fluid to flow into the third leaf.

I was assigned to the *Export Builder* from the fall of 1969 to the spring of 1970. During that period the vessel made three round trips to the Far East, calling at Hong Kong, Taiwan, Korea, and four ports in Japan. On her return to the United States, she would call at San Francisco, Los Angeles, and San Juan, Puerto Rico, before returning to New York.

I dated a woman in Rockport between trips during the following winter. After a few trips, however, I suppose she grew tired of my absences, and by spring the courtship had ended. Again, in accordance with my usual routine of sailing during the winter and spending summers at home in Rockport, I arrived home in the spring with my pockets full of cash and ready for a good time. I suppose that I was a little careless with the way that I handled this money after having been paid off. I remember walking through large, dark, deserted warehouses with cash stuffed in my pockets and in my shoes. It did not occur to me that the longshoremen working on the piers were well aware of when ships paid off. I could have been attacked and robbed of the fruits of several months at sea. Fortunately, it did not happen. On one flight home, as I settled into my seat on the plane I realized that the smallest bills that I had in my pockets were one hundred dollar notes. When the flight attendant came down the aisle to collect the fare, I carefully peeled off one of them and told her that I was sorry that it was the smallest that I had. She replied, "If that is the smallest, I would like to see the biggest." Perhaps she was looking for a good time.

I prepared my sailboat for a summer of sailing and good times. Having the means to be able to buy the equipment and materials that I needed for my boat and still have plenty of money to enjoy the time at home made me really feel as though all that time at sea was worthwhile. I was also able to assist my parents with some financial difficulties that they had encountered during the time that I was at sea.

THE SUMMER THAT CHANGED MY LIFE

Shortly after arriving home that summer, while enjoying a few beers with an old high school friend, I mentioned that I had not met any "new" girls since returning from the Far East. He grinned and said that he would be driving to the White Mountains in New Hampshire the following day with his girlfriend and three of her friends, who had moved from the Midwest to Cape Ann for the summer. He added that they intended to hike most of the day in the mountains and then have a cookout at the girls' camp after returning to Rockport. He made it clear that I was welcome to join them if I so wished. I told him that I wasn't sure if I would go because I had recently glued the mast of my sailboat and still had some work to do on it at the yacht club. We agreed, upon his insistence, that he would bring the girls to the yacht club and introduce me to them. They came to the yacht club early the next morning and, after meeting them, I decided to go hiking and relegated the boat plans to another time.

One of the girls, especially, drew my attention early in the day as we drove to New Hampshire. We listened to the music of the Beatles and had a good time getting to know one another in the car. It was a beautiful day, and the scenery was breathtaking as we hiked past waterfalls and scenic mountain vistas. The name of the girl that cornered my attention was Sally, and she lived in the town of Park Forest, Illinois. We hit it off right away and spent most of the day together in conversation.

The three girls lived in a small New England cottage not far from *my home. After returning to Rockport, we enjoyed a great cookout in their backyard, during which Sally and I stole away and got to know one another even more, a perfect ending to a most enjoyable day. She had never been on a sailboat before coming to Cape Ann and did not realize what the summer ahead would be like. I asked her if she wanted to be my crew, and she signed on with great enthusiasm. We raced every weekend for the entire summer, and our relationship continued to grow stronger. I was so proud to introduce her to all of my yacht club friends.*

As September drew near, I began thinking about going back to sea. My career was another thing that Sally had no knowledge of, and I was apprehensive to think that she might not be able to adjust to the long periods of separation. We had not discussed marriage at that point, but it was certainly in the back of my mind. I returned to the Export Buyer, *which was bound to the Far East, and Sally returned to her home in Illinois. We kept in touch with each other all that winter, and it seemed to me as though our relationship was getting to the point where we might want to spend the rest of our lives together. I made three trips that winter on board the* Export Buyer, *about nine months in all. At the end of the third trip I was very anxious to go on vacation so that I could go to Park Forest and meet Sally's family and friends.*

On the day of the ship's return, we were due to pay off in New York for the entire trip. The process involved the shipping commissioner boarding the vessel accompanied by armed guards and a satchel full of cash. The crew then lined up outside the captain's office. When each crewmember's name was called he would enter and receive his wages in cash. There were very few women working on ships at that time. I stood my cargo watch that morning and was anxiously awaiting the payoff in the afternoon.

While on cargo watch, I was twisting the turnbuckle on a wire pendant using a piece of wood in order to pull the second leaf of the hatch cover closer to the bulkhead. As I pulled the wood toward me, it snapped in half, and a wood sliver struck my right eyebrow, leaving a deep gash. It was a nasty looking wound, which resulted in a large amount of bleeding. With the payoff in mind, I wanted to avoid treatment ashore, so I went directly to my room and looked into a mirror, trying to assess the situation. After close examination, I decided to shave the eyebrow and, using plastic sutures, pull the wound together. I was successful enough to stem the bleeding so that I would not miss the payoff.

As I look back on the moment that I called Sally, I realize that I could have used a better choice of words. During our conversation I told her that I did not look quite as I did the last time she had seen me. She, of course, had no idea what I was talking about at the time. My plane arrived in O'Hare Airport that evening, and I took the commuter bus to Park Forest for my long-awaited visit with Sally. The next day I went to see a doctor for treatment of the eye injury. He asked who had treated the wound on the previous day. When I told him I had done it myself while looking into a mirror, he replied, "I could not have done it better myself." After I told him what had happened, he said that I was very fortunate not to have sustained a serious eye injury.

My visit with Sally and her family did more to convince me that there was a strong possibility our relationship could build to the point of marriage. When I told Sally that I might go back to sea again, she was surprised and said that she might go to Europe. The thought of her traveling to Europe and possibly meeting a handsome European man made me so nervous that I made a very impulsive decision. I resigned from American Export-Isbrandtsen Lines upon returning to the East Coast and arranged for my gear to be taken off the ship and sent to Rockport. I mistakenly assumed that Sally would not marry someone who would be away for two-thirds of the year. After spending several weeks at home, the realization hit me that I was unemployed and would have to find a job. I began to have second thoughts about the wisdom of my decision.

LAUNCH OPERATOR

A local yacht club in Manchester, Massachusetts was in need of a launch operator, so I applied for the position, based upon my small-boat experience. The club captain, Carl, was a huge man with a winning personality who became one of my best friends. After an initial interview with the club commodore and some test runs in each of the two launches, I was hired. The hours were long during weekdays, usually from 0800 to 1900, and could extend even longer on Saturdays and Sundays. On the weekends it wasn't unusual to be caught during a busy time without a break for hours. I met many interesting people while I was employed at the club.

One member owned a beautiful sail auxiliary vessel with a wide assortment of electronic antennas mounted on the mast. On the morning of the Fourth of July, as I was transporting him to his boat, I heard someone tell us to look down the channel. I turned and, much to my surprise saw four fighter jets streaming toward us at high speed. Passing over our heads, they turned upward and climbed straight into the sky. I looked toward the stern of the launch, and my passenger smilingly said, "That's ok, George, they do that for me every Fourth of July." Only then did I learn that he was the Secretary of the Air Force.

In addition to operating the launches, launch operators were responsible for maintaining the boats to rigid standards. One fact about varnishing has been embedded in my brain ever since my association with my friend Carl. He once said to me, "If you can't get the varnishing done by early afternoon, don't even attempt it." It is good advice, because I learned that a good varnish project might be totally ruined by late afternoon dampness. The younger members of the club loved Carl so much that they presented

him with a golden retriever puppy, which he named Maggie. My fondness for golden retrievers dates to this time, and I knew that I would have one someday.

It was a challenge to learn the names of each launch passenger and the names of their boats. A respected and well-liked elderly man name Henry, who had worked at the club for many years, filled in as launch operator when we became really busy. He never said a bad word about anyone. I remember whenever a friend had passed on, he would say "Too bad, poor bugger."

On slow days we broke up the monotony of sitting around on the porch by dreaming up pranks. Carl made a huge slingshot from surgical tubing and flat rubber sheets, with a slab of leather in the middle. The club awning was attached to a pipe frame around the perimeter of the porch, and each end of the sling was attached to one of these pipes. When a club member passed in front of the dock on his boat, one of us would place a balloon filled with water into the leather pouch, and we'd pull back the sling as far as possible. We became deadly accurate with our shots after some practice. Not to be outdone, the boat owners designed even more efficient means to send water balloons back at us.

Carl passed away at much too young an age, but his memory will always live on in my mind. He died peacefully in his sleep, for which I am grateful. Not long ago, I had occasion to ride one of the yacht club's launches to a friend's boat, and when I read the name Carl Magee on the bow of the approaching launch, I was emotionally moved. It is such a fitting tribute for the club to have named one of their shipshape launches after such a kind, capable, likable person. The same is true of Henry, for whom the other launch was named.

SUMMER 1971

During the summer of 1971, I lived in an apartment above a gift shop known as the Pewter Shop. The shop was owned and operated by a local craftsman named Lawson Murch, who was extremely skilled at shaping pewter bowls, plates, cups and many other items by hand. Mr. Murch has recently passed on, but the shop continues to thrive. It is now managed and owned by Lawson's son and a good friend of mine named Chris Murch. Sally returned to Rockport and rented a room in a home owned by an elderly woman, whose son is a good friend of mine. We enjoyed another summer of parties, yacht club activities, and sailing when I wasn't at work driving the launch. There was a deck attached to my apartment, upon which I spent many hours watching the tourists pass by below. As I drove the launch, I pondered how I was going to put my seagoing expertise to good use for the future. I never enjoyed the process of looking for a job, so I avoided it whenever possible.

One day, as Sally and I were considering my employment options for the future, I asked her if she would like to be married to a fireman or a mailman. She immediately responded with, "Am I to take that as a proposal?" I replied in the affirmative, though it was not how I had envisioned making my proposal. When she said, "Yes, I thought you would never ask," I was excited beyond words. The thought that we were going to spend the rest of our lives together really was something!

GRADUATE SCHOOL

The launch job ended in early fall, and it was time make a decision about my future now that going to sea was not in the cards, at least for the moment. I was having considerable difficulty finding a specific career path. Ocean Engineering, the study of the design and construction of offshore oilrigs and other underwater structures, sounded interesting. I learned about the Ocean Engineering program at the University of Massachusetts graduate school and decided to look into it. After applying for admission, I was provisionally accepted on the condition that I achieve A and B grades, thanks to one professor who had sponsored me. I found the engineering subjects interesting and excelled in them. The plan was for me to complete the course in two years. It quickly became apparent that the process was going to take much longer than originally intended. I decided to resign from the program and pursue another course of action.

While I attended the University of Massachusetts in Amherst, Massachusetts, Sally taught a special education class of six students in a public school nearby. We lived in an area different from what either of us was accustomed to. The apartment building was located along the banks of the Connecticut River, where tobacco was the primary crop for the local farmers. I felt out of my element there, away from the ocean. After resigning from graduate school I held down several part-time jobs until Sally finished her teaching contract in June.

RUSSIAN ODYSSEY

By January 1972, Sally and I were thinking about our upcoming wedding in Park Forest, Illinois, and making the necessary plans for the ceremony. Neither of us had any preference where our honeymoon should be. One evening we were invited to dinner with Charlie and Jill, the couple who had introduced us initially in 1970, and another couple. The conversation turned to the subject of travel. Charlie had learned that the Russian government was opening its borders to foreign tourists, and he and Jill wanted to travel to a country to which few United States citizens had journeyed. He had researched the possibility of camping in Russia, and he said that it was possible.

As the conversation continued over several glasses of wine, Sally and I decided that Russia might make an interesting honeymoon destination for us. All six of us finally agreed that a trip to Russia was appealing and that we should begin making plans to go together. "What a great adventure," we thought, six Americans traveling behind the Iron Curtain during the cold war. None of us could have predicted how much of an adventure it was going to be. We planned to rent a minibus and stay at campsites along the route. We presented our travel itinerary for approval three months in advance, but the Russian authorities held the itinerary for several months before returning it with slight modifications. We were required to specify where we would stop each night, which was difficult given that we had no knowledge of road conditions. Finally the trip itinerary was *firmed up, the necessary gear was gathered, and we were ready to go.*

Following our wedding, Sally and I traveled to the Indiana dunes on the shores of Lake Michigan to spend some time alone before beginning our upcoming odyssey to the Soviet Union. We were the last to leave our wedding reception, and it was late when we arrived at our motel in Michigan. Upon our arrival, we were told that our room had been given to someone else. After finally getting a room, we turned in, exhausted, after a beautiful, fun-filled day. Early the following morning, I awoke and walked out to view the lake, only to be greeted by the stench of rotten fish that closely resembled the smell of the old de-hydration fish processing plant on the Gloucester waterfront. Looking out at the lake, we observed thousands of dead fish floating in the water and on the sand. This was the result, apparently, of a huge alewife kill, an occurrence that had been becoming more and more common in recent years, according to Sally. In spite of that, we frolicked on the dunes, hiked, and relaxed for the weekend.

Upon our return to Rockport, we firmed up our arrangements to leave for the Soviet Union. As the departure time drew closer we had mixed feelings about this bold adventure. We boarded a plane to London and then flew on to Vienna, where our vehicle was reserved. The next day we picked up the minibus, packed our gear, and headed out toward the border of Czechoslovakia. The border crossing was traumatic for us all, because we were unused to seeing heavy weapons carried by deadly serious border guards. Early in the day, as we drove along on a rough dirt road, we pulled into a parking area next to a café seeking a cup of coffee. While we were there I struck up a conversation with one of the villagers. At some point during the conversation, the man said, "Kennedy good, Policia no good!" That was the extent of our ability to communicate in Czech. That evening we slept in a cottage deep in a valley between two mountain ranges. It was an idyllic setting, situated near a cold stream of pristine fresh water flowing down the mountainside. We were excited to begin our trip with such a pleasant experience, but it was downhill all the way from there. When we crossed the border into Poland, we were required to drive the minibus over a man-made trench for a contraband search. None of us had entertained the thought that someone might have attempted to smuggle contraband under the vehicle. As we passed over a trench, armed guards searched the undercarriage but found nothing, much to our relief.

In Poland we encountered hot, dusty, and difficult traveling over rough dirt roads. On our application to the in-tourist agency we had been required to estimate our daily travel times between specified tent sites, but the estimates were way off the mark because we did not appreciate the difficulty of each day's travel. One morning we encountered a farmer, who had tipped his hay wagon over in the middle of the narrow dirt road causing a huge traffic backup while he pitched the spilled hay back into the wagon. Sally and I had never camped and slept in a tent. This added to the list of challenges that we faced each day. Frequently we resorted to sleeping in the back of the minibus. Marketplaces were dirty, and little fresh food was available. Often we noticed flies crawling over the meat in the dirty stalls of the vendors. After several days in Poland, we crossed the border into Russia. The people seemed depressed wherever we went, and the houses in the villages were dingy and colorless. As we walked down a main street in Kiev, a man approached me from behind and asked, "You are American?" I replied that we were, and he responded with, "You are very lucky, you have only happiness. We have nothing but tears."

While we were there, I developed an ear infection and attempted to obtain medical treatment. After finding an in-tourist guide, I was able to locate a hospital. The outside was gray and resembled a warehouse. Once inside, I fell into line to await treatment, only to be confronted by an obese Russian woman who angrily made it clear that I had cut in front of her. I eventually got to see a female doctor, also obese, who spoke no English. Since I spoke no Russian, I knew I was in for a challenge. She examined my ear and attempted to describe the problem, but became frustrated at our inability to communicate. She pointed at the red T-shirt I was wearing and then to my ear, and I understood that my ear was red and infected.

She then made a gesture as if she was drinking whiskey and said "Schnapps" several times, attempting to instruct me to treat it with alcohol.

On my day to drive, I noticed that the road was deteriorating to a rough surface with many ruts. It was clear that I had made a wrong turn, and we were lost. Soon a Russian police car approached us rapidly from behind, and we became fearful that we would be arrested for trespassing or some other offense. We stopped, and the officers asked us, in Russian, if we were all right, or something to that effect. We were relieved to discover that they were only trying to help. All during the trip, we were constantly aware that the police were never far away. The dangers of traveling in a communist country were all too clear.

It was difficult to cook at the campsites, because it was necessary to build a fire and heat water before beginning to cook our freeze-dried food. The sanitary conditions at the campsites were terrible, especially inside the public bathrooms. Eventually we crossed into Romania and began passing many brightly painted houses with beautiful flowers in the yards. The Rumanian people we encountered while passing through their villages seemed very happy compared with those in Russia. Eventually we passed into Hungary and were beginning to look forward to the end of our adventurous odyssey. By this time we were tired of living in tents and traveling over substandard roads. As we walked the streets of Budapest, I noticed that the Hotel Budapest had a Master Card sign in the window, and I immediately suggested that we book rooms for the night. The others needed no convincing, so we all checked in, relieved at the prospect of sleeping in real beds with clean sheets. That night we feasted on rich Hungarian food, and all of us became sick, whether from food poisoning or the sudden shift in our diet we couldn't be sure. The trip was a learning experience, and it renewed our appreciation for the freedoms and comforts we experience every day in the United States.

SETTLING INTO MARRIED LIFE

After returning from our honeymoon to Eastern Europe, Sally and I settled down in a little cottage in Rockport. I returned to my position as launch operator, and Sally found a position at a private school working with children with dyslexia. The summer involved long hours at work and many social engagements, but as fall approached, I found myself facing the ever-present challenge of another job search. I still was not sure of what career I might follow ashore, and I was beginning to feel that the easy way out was to return to sea. I tried to find a compromise job that would enable me to use my seagoing skills yet remain close to home, but as I was searching for such a position, we began to feel some financial pressure. Searching for a way to bring in cash in addition to the several local jobs I was working, I decided to sell my much-valued sextant. It was an impulsive move, one to which Sally objected strongly, but I insisted, and the sextant was sold.

I must jump ahead in my career narrative to relate a positive ending to the sale of the sextant story. Some thirty-four years later, I was waiting to get a haircut in front of Sal's, my favorite barbershop, when I began a conversation with a gentleman regarding my plan to teach navigation. He stated that he had purchased a sextant from a man who was captain of a schooner called the When and If. By that time I had been one of the captains of that boat, but I did not realize at first that he was referring to me. I began to name the captains who had preceded me in command of the When and If, and suddenly

I realized that I had found my long lost sextant! Excited to have located it at long last, I suggested that I buy it from him, and to my delight, he agreed. That evening Sally and I went to his home to examine it, and I gave him the cash. I recall how happy and relieved I was to have this prized instrument home again. I took it to a nautical instruments shop to have it appraised and checked for error, and it is now sitting in my office, where I can look at it and ponder the days when I depended upon it to navigate my way around the world. I recently took it to a nearby beach and worked out a noon latitude sight that came pretty close to my actual latitude.

CAPTAIN OF AN OIL BARGE

While searching for local work on the water, I discovered that a captain holding a certificate as first class pilot upon the local waters was needed for a small, self-propelled oil barge. I would have to obtain another license in addition to my Third Mate License. Twelve round trips as an observer upon the waters in question, were required prior to being examined for the license as pilot. After satisfying this requirement I passed the examination and obtained a license as First Class Pilot of Tank Vessels of 100 gross tons. One deckhand was required in addition to the captain, in accordance with United States Coast Guard licensing requirements. At the initial interview I was informed that the boat was undergoing repairs and would be in the shipyard for several weeks. Upon being offered the position, I was asked to fill a temporary position until the overhaul of the barge was completed. Upon reporting to work, I found that the temporary position was as manager of a truck stop that serviced large tractor-trailer trucks. After having discharged their cargoes of meat from the Midwest, the trucks proceeded to a small port, which was five miles from my home, for cleaning prior to being loaded with cartons of frozen fish. Fifty-pound cartons packed with blocks of quick-frozen fish and crabmeat had been shipped into port aboard small break-bulk ships and stored in large warehouses along the waterfront. After the trucks were cleaned, the cargo was loaded for the return trip to the Midwest. Instead of managing the facility, I learned that I would pressure-wash trailers to rid them of the blood and guts that remained after the meat had been unloaded. I persevered through this ordeal for several weeks until the vessel was ready for service.

The oil barge was used to fuel fishing vessels, factory ships, small freighters, and yachts. Many of the freighters hailed from the Faroe Islands, Iceland, and Newfoundland laden with cargoes of frozen fish. Two of these small freighters, *Blue Peter* and *Blue Trader*, were the vessels in which I had voyaged to Newfoundland as a Sea Scout. The barge was diesel powered and approximately sixty feet long. Fuel oil was loaded on board via an adjustable loading arm mounted on the company dock. Drums of lube-oil, rags, and other commodities were carried as deck cargo when special ordered by the customer.

Several fishing vessels docked at the company dock on a regular basis. Often more than one of these fishing vessels returned to port at the same time after a long trip, loaded with fish. It was important for each vessel to receive the fuel as soon as possible so that the accounts could be settled and the crew paid for the voyage. Each would post a crewmember on the bow holding up a fish, yelling, "You fuel me first, I give you halibut!" or, "You fuel me first, I give you haddock!" I took home plenty of fresh fish as a result of that job. On one occasion a chief engineer from one of the ships gave me a fifty-pound box of frozen crabmeat.

A Japanese freighter once deployed an oil boom outside my vessel after I had docked alongside. I didn't feel that this was necessary, but it seemed like a wise precaution. Shortly after the floating boom had been deployed, I noticed oil on the surface of the water drifting toward me, and surrounding the barge. I observed a Coast Guard helicopter, circling overhead, and was glad that the boom was in place. The water around me was perfectly clean, but a thick sheen of oil had formed outside the boom.

I operated this barge for a year, by which time it was clear to me that this was not what I wanted to continue doing. It was a temporary measure to garner some income until I found something more in keeping with my abilities and qualifications.

THE PILOT BOAT *CAN DO* TRAGEDY

I will pause at this time in my narrative to relate an incident that occurred during the Blizzard of 1978. The port of Gloucester has sustained the loss of thousands of fishermen over the years. The names of these men and others lost at sea are preserved in a permanent monument located on the Boulevard, near the famous Fisherman at the Wheel. Frank Quirk and four other brave souls perished during the Blizzard of '78 attempting to come to the aid of those in need, and their names are included on this monument. This is a brief review of the incident, which has been chronicled in a book entitled *Ten Hours Until Dawn*, by Michael J. Tougias.

While working on the oil barge, I met Frank Quirk, who owned the pilot boat *Can Do*. She was used to transport pilots to and from ships calling at Salem and Gloucester. He was proud of his boat and often described how well she performed in heavy seas. Frank was well liked on the Gloucester waterfront. He had an outgoing personality and was always there to lend a hand when needed. During the Blizzard of '78, a tanker ran aground on a reef outside Salem Harbor, and the captain called the Coast Guard for assistance, stating that his vessel was taking on water. Frank and four of his friends listened to the voice traffic between the stricken vessel and the Coast Guard, and they were still listening as they returned to the *Can Do*, thinking they might be able to assist in some way. By this time two utility boats had been dispatched from the Coast Guard base, and both had suffered severe damage from the heavy seas, which had built to tremendous heights. One made it back safely, but the other had lost all electronics and needed assistance. Frank got on the radio with an offer to help and readied the *Can Do* for whatever was needed.

They headed for sea to locate the stricken Coast Guard vessel, and as soon as the vessel rounded Dog Bar Breakwater, it had to have become apparent to those on board that this was going to be a long and grueling night. Shortly after leaving port, the *Can Do* was disabled and was reduced to one battery-powered radio for communication. A ham radio operator, traveling along the shore, recorded the transmissions during that long night's ordeal. I have heard portions of the tape recording of the voice transmissions during the last hours of the *Can Do*, and it made my blood run cold.

Overwhelmed by the power of the huge seas, the *Can Do* ran onto a reef and sank in the vicinity of Marblehead. The bodies of her crew were eventually recovered, as was the hull. The stricken Coast Guard craft found its way safely to port. The tanker crew remained on board after it was determined that the ship was in no immediate danger of sinking. The captain apparently did not realize at the time of the initial call that the vessel was actually aground. Salvage crews eventually were able to refloat the tanker and tow it to a nearby shipyard for repairs.

My sincere sympathy goes out to the relatives of those who were on board the *Can Do* and gave their lives in the attempt to save the lives of others. It has been a long recognized custom that mariners will go to the aid of others when in need. Nowhere is this custom better demonstrated than in a situation such as the one described above.

COASTAL TANKERS

After one year on the oil barge, I contacted a marine transportation company operating a fleet of small coastal tankers along the New England coast, and was assigned as chief officer of several vessels upon the waters of Massachusetts Bay, with an occasional voyage to the Maine Coast.

One of these small tankers transited a tidal inlet flowing from sea to a small fuel depot located approximately five miles inland. Navigating a vessel in this river was particularly challenging due to its winding course and shallow waters. One of the first navigational challenges encountered was a narrow railroad bridge. Safe passage depended upon the ability of the deckhand to quickly secure a springline to a piling, without which the vessel would be unable to make the necessary sharp turn to line up for the narrow bridge opening. A good deckhand who could accurately throw a line around a piling was essential for this operation. Several similar bridges were encountered before finally reaching the discharge terminal, and the vessel often made contact with the bridge timbers as we traversed the openings. The crew consisted of seven men and an excellent cook, whose meals contributed to a very large weight gain for me during that time period.

Another of these tankers regularly transited the Penobscot River after passing through the harbor at Bucksport, Maine. Navigation frequently involved lining up trees with church steeples and other manmade and natural objects for guidance due to the scarcity of government aids. The passage up Penobscot Bay to Bucksport took us past Castine Harbor and Maine Maritime Academy, my old stomping grounds.

One slightly larger vessel was used primarily along the Maine Coast. One day I was at home working in the basement when I received a telephone call from a company representative requesting that I immediately come on board but offering no details as to the length of the voyage to Maine. After reporting to the captain, I helped finish the loading process, and the vessel sailed for Portland, Maine. I stood one navigation watch from midnight to six in the morning and turned in. The deckhand called me at noon and said that I would be leaving on the next bus to Boston. I was confused at first, but after a while it became clear that a person who held the necessary certification for offshore waters between Cape Ann and Portland, Maine, had been required for the overnight passage.

I had left the house so quickly on the previous day that I had forgotten to bring house keys. No one was home when I returned, but I remembered that the bedroom windows were unlocked. I located the aluminum ladder in the yard, extended it against the side of the house, deftly opened the second-floor window, and entered the bedroom on my stomach. I fully expected one of the neighbors to report a burglary to the police, but all was well and I was not reported.

I continued to change my positions of employment as I struggled to determine what direction to pursue. I kept trying to convince myself that I could find a shore job, but eventually I realized that I was trained for a maritime career, and that was going to be the direction I would seek. But first I tried one more avenue, which sounded interesting and challenging.

THE *WHEN AND IF*

During the spring of 1974 I became captain of an auxiliary sail-training schooner named *When and If*. My association with the *When and If* had begun many years before, when, as a boy of ten, I had crewed on a gaff-rigged ketch named *Scylla* that carried tourists on sailing excursions on the waters of Sandy Bay. The *Scylla's* captain later became the private captain of the *When and If*.

An incident had occurred while sailing *Scylla* off Halibut Point that was embarrassing for a ten-year old boy. As we were sailing with our rail down, I went below and noticed water coming into the cabin from a leaking pipefitting which passed through the hull. It had already reached a depth of two to three inches above the cabin floor by the time it was discovered. Not knowing what to do, I quickly made my way up the companionway ladder to notify the captain, and yelled that we were sinking! The passengers grew apprehensive and wondered if they were in danger. Later, the captain told me that I should not have done this, as it resulted in having to give a refund to each of the passengers.

When I was in high school, I was asked to crew on the *When and If* with the same captain who had skippered the *Scylla*. I was wildly excited to have this opportunity to cruise all summer in the waters of Maine and Canada, but my parents wouldn't allow me to go. They never did fully explain their reasoning, but perhaps they thought I was too young. In any event, I was extremely disappointed to miss an opportunity to experience the world beyond Rockport on a large schooner.

When and If was designed by the John G. Alden yacht design firm and built by the FF Pendleton yard in Wiscasset, Maine in 1939 for General George S. Patton. Following the death of General Patton, the *When and If* was passed on to other family members. *When and If* sailed out of Manchester, Massachusetts for most of her early life. In 1972 she was donated to a local school for children with special needs. The headmaster of the school envisioned the benefits that the students would gain from being part of a sail-training program. While Sally was in charge of admissions at the school she learned that a captain was needed for *When and If*. Being familiar with my sailing background and my historical connection with the boat, Sally knew that I was the man for the position. After a few telephone conversations I was called in for an interview and hired very soon after.

Once again I was being given the opportunity to sail on the *When and If*, but this time as captain. The initial challenge was to become familiar with the boat's handling characteristics. I contacted the previous captain, who had requested me as crew years before, and asked if he would like to join me in the shakedown sail. When he appeared on the day of our sail, his eyes lit up at the sight of the boat. Although it had been years since he had sailed her, he handled her as if he had never left her. I watched his every move, because I knew that from then on she was going to be my total responsibility.

The *When and If* is sixty-five feet long and is rigged with a gaff foresail and Marconi main. Students sailed on board for the day and for extended cruises along the coast of Maine. In order to provide them with an opportunity to gain maximum experience while handling her under sail, students were trained to sail her to and from the mooring whenever possible. Routine maintenance on the boat was carried out at the mooring or at the local boatyard. Over a span of three years, I stripped the bottom, topsides, and conducted a complete overhaul of the masts and rigging. An elaborate wood-and-canvas shelter, which was erected over the boat, enabled me to work half the day during winter. Students attended a course, which I designed and taught, that combined boat handling, knot tying, weather, sailing, and environmental science in the afternoon during the winter months. Whenever the *When and If* sailed on summer cruises, the students were divided into three groups. Seamanship and navigation was taught to one group while the other two groups received tutoring from two trained teachers.

The approach to the boatyard dock was a challenging one. It was necessary to steer past the float into a small turning basin. One busy summer day as I entered the turning basin and began to do my turn, I noticed an older couple sitting on their boat at the mooring enjoying late afternoon cocktails. They were not aware that it was necessary for me to pass the bowsprit so close to them that it seemed as though it would pass over their heads. I completed my turn and went on to position the boat at the boatyard float. About ten minutes later a man approached with two cocktails in hand, one for him and one for me. He said that he admired the way I was able to turn the *When and If*. He admitted that he and his wife thought that I was going to do damage to their boat with the bowsprit. What neither of them realized was the fact that the boat's propeller was so large and that the pitch adjusted when put in reverse. This gave the effect of having a stern thruster that pushed the stern to port at a right angle to the boat's heading. It was necessary to turn to starboard in that situation because of this characteristic. Because it was the end of my workday and I was going straight home, I took the man up on his offer of an afternoon cocktail.

The vessel took part in a coastal race as part of Operation Sail in Newport, Rhode Island, in 1976. The course of the race took us from Newport, through Long Island Sound to a turning buoy, and back to Cleveland Ledge Light in Buzzards Bay, eventually returning to finish off Newport. Fog shut in just before we entered Buzzards Bay, at which point I contemplated dropping out of the race. I had radar, however, so in the excitement of the moment I elected to continue. This turned out to be a bad decision, because a short time later the radar ceased to operate, forcing us to navigate by dead reckoning. The return trip to Newport through treacherous waters, tracking our position with estimates based on speed through the water, current, and wind, was extremely stressful and not without its share of problems.

I am proud to have had the opportunity to be captain of such a beautiful boat. I often took her to Sandy Bay so that my friends could see her, because she made a picturesque sight anchored off Front Beach on a late summer afternoon. On one trip I decided to dock her at the end of T Wharf in Rockport, near the yacht club, where I recalled there being lots of water when I was a child. I docked the *When and If* alongside at high water, knowing that the boat would ground out at low water but not fully appreciating what was ahead. As the water level dropped, the boat began to list away from the dock, and I secured a line to a piling as a precaution. The situation rapidly became embarrassing, and I decided to cover up for my misfortune by rigging our small boat and telling friends that I was cleaning the bottom. I am not sure they believed my story, but I tried anyway.

One afternoon, while sailing from Camden, Maine, for Port Clyde, I could not start the diesel engine. I called a friend and asked her to arrange for a mechanic to meet us for repairs upon our arrival in Port Clyde, but the harbor's narrow entrance channel presented a challenge. With the wind out of the northwest, we would have to tack against the wind all the way up the channel. We practiced raising and lowering the sails all day and became very proficient as a team. Our entrance was successful, and we came to anchor right off the Port Clyde town dock. My friend came out with the mechanic, and the repairs were completed.The school operated the *When and If* until the mid 1980s, at which time the vessel broke away from her mooring and went aground in Manchester Harbor. She was declared a total loss by the insurance company but has since been totally rebuilt and is sailing today. The quarters have been modified, and she is now painted her original black hull color. Recently, while anchored in the Hudson River on board a tugboat, I noticed a large sailing vessel coming up the river, and it turned out to be the *When and If*. It was good to see her once again.

MARRIED LIFE AND A SEAGOING CAREER

In the early days of sail, mariners were often separated from their families for years at a time. Many marriages failed due to the double burden placed upon the wife and mother of the children at home and the extremely long periods of separation. The challenge of raising children and maintaining the home was much more difficult then. Frequently, the wives and children of ships' masters lived on board in order to avoid the separation issue. Many masters' wives gave birth to several children while on extended voyages.

I have spoken to persons who feel that having a husband and father going to sea could negatively influence the process of raising a family. The years have proven to me that this is not so, however, as Sally and I have raised two daughters successfully. Between voyages I was able to spend large amounts of quality time with my wife and two daughters, Kirsten and Katelyn. Indeed, the merchant mariner's available time to be with family exceeds that afforded by a more conventional job ashore. The shore worker has weekends free and, perhaps, a two-week vacation once a year to spend time at home. Mariners most often work "day for day," which apportions equal time at home and at sea. When Sally and I were married, seamen worked about two-thirds time at sea and one-third at home. Most people in the workforce have to contend with the challenge of performing everyday chores and errands, attending social engagements, and still doing the work at home on weekends. I had the opportunity to go on frequent family trips without feeling stressed about what had to be done at home. I had more than enough time between trips to catch up on work around the house and complete those projects that needed to be done.

While I was assigned as chief officer on board oil tankers making voyages on the West Coast of the United States, my family and I lived apart as much as three months at a time. Between trips, my time at home usually amounted to a month and a half, during which I completed necessary repairs and projects around the house. If I chose not to work at home, I often went on day trips with my family. This life in no way impeded my ability to maintain a healthy and nurturing father-daughter relationship. Sally and I conversed every five or six days on the telephone, except in cases of extra-long voyages, when we talked more frequently.

Today, the ability to communicate by cellular telephone and electronic mail has brought the mariner and his loved ones much closer than ever before. In some cases, ships are equipped with satellite communications, which, although expensive, allows mariners to keep in touch with their families on long voyages when no other means of contact is available. I do not miss standing in line at the phone booth on the dock, waiting for crewmembers of other vessels to finish their conversations.

Even with these improvements, marital relationships often dissolve for one reason or another. Most often it is because the wife is insecure and in need of constant companionship from her spouse. This insecurity all too often leads to her seeking companionship with other men, eventually leading to the breakup of the relationship. I have seen many of my shipmates' marriages end up in divorce because their relationships lacked the most basic ingredient for success—namely, trust. If either party distrusts the other, the relationship cannot survive a seagoing life. There are situations today in which both the husband and wife have seagoing careers and go to sea. I wonder about the logistics of this type of arrangement.

One thing that Sally has noticed while traveling on business is the reaction she gets from other wives when she tells them what I do for employment. When they ask what I do, she replies that I am gone for half the year working aboard a tugboat. The reply is almost invariably, "Wow, I would give anything to have my husband away for half the year!" The separation can be a good thing, because it allows a husband and wife an opportunity to pursue their own goals and be independent.

Both parties must talk openly and share their feelings. When it became apparent that Sally and I were to become husband and wife, I struggled with how to handle my career, fearing that Sally was unprepared for this type of life. It was this fear that led me to resign from the company that then employed me. In retrospect, I understand that I should have explained the advantages and disadvantages to my future wife before taking that impulsive decision. Many years after our marriage, I returned to sea on other assignments and found that she was able to maintain her life professionally and was perfectly able to care for the children. I have not encountered a more caring and compassionate person. I notice and admire her many fine qualities every day, whether it be her unyielding patience and understanding of our family issues or knowing how to get me to leave the kitchen without hurting my feelings. (She and I do not work well together in the kitchen.)

How well I remember the times when I left home for months at sea, only to find, when I unpacked my bag on the ship, little notes reminding me of her love and wishes for a safe voyage. My advice to anyone considering a seagoing life is to keep the lines of communication open and make the most of the time you have together. Most importantly, trust is the most essential ingredient in maintaining a healthy relationship while enduring long periods of separation.

MY OTHER LIFE

Approximately one year after Sally and I were married, we purchased a small cape in Rockport that had been built in 1867. We were excited to have found a home within walking distance of town and the waterfront. The property was bordered on three sides by natural fieldstone walls, which had been built by farmers while clearing the fields for planting. The cellar—dark and musty, with a dirt floor—was accessed by a narrow and rickety stairway. On its far side was a square concrete area, which had been used to store coal for the original coal-fired furnace. There were always projects to do with an old house, and I enjoyed doing the work required to keep the property looking nice.

One of my most challenging projects was jacking up the back of the house in order to replace the cinder block foundation. A large, rotten beam, very much in need of replacement, stretched across the back of the house. It had been supported by stone and mortared pillars at only three points and was sagging to the point of collapsing. A local contractor friend coached me every step of the way, first suggesting that I rent hydraulic jacks and the other equipment necessary to complete the job. After weeks of skinned knuckles and exhausting days, we began to show progress. I enlisted the aid of a local mason to help me rebuild the foundation, and soon we had in place a new, pressure-treated wooden sill supported by a new concrete block foundation across the back of the house. I was proud *to have completed the biggest part of the job myself. I had redone the countertop in the kitchen just a few months prior to embarking on the block foundation project, and during the jacking process, I would take a few turns on a screw jack and then hurry into the kitchen to check the level of the counter. It was amazing to see just how much the shape of the house could be changed by a few turns of the screw jack.*

I built a rough wooden fence for privacy in back of the house, using boards from my grandfather's old barn. I called on a friend, and together we spent weeks completing that project. We lived in the High Street house between 1973 and 1979. Due to its advanced age, our little house was always in need of tender loving care. The storm windows were the sash type, requiring a ladder to fasten them from the outside with screws after inserting felt strips for insulation. I built a wall unit in an upstairs back room for our books, a TV, and a sewing table. The hedge in front of the house had wide gaps showing little or no growth, and in my quest for information on what to do about this problem, I read an article on how to trim a hedge way back. One day as Sally was leaving for work I told her that I was going to trim the front hedge. She agreed, and I went ahead as planned. When she returned home, she was shocked to find most of the hedge gone. She had not expected such a drastic step. It was sometime after that before I did another landscaping project without first explaining to her thoroughly beforehand what I was about to do.While we were living on High Street, we adopted a mixed-breed dog named Maggie. Unfortunately, we did not put enough effort into training her, and she gave us trouble later with behavior issues. One night as we were preparing dinner, I removed some baked stuffed haddock from the oven and set it on the countertop. While I was greeting guests at the front door, Maggie was being very quiet, and upon entering the kitchen I found the reason for her silence. She had stood on her hind legs and eaten most of the dinner. Sally put something together for our guests and left Maggie's leftovers for me. The next addition to our happy home on High Street was our first daughter, Kirsten Dana Grimes, who was born on July 24, 1975. As an infant, Kirsten was so active that I had to adjust the mattress of her crib to its lowest setting. Once when I went into her room, I found her lying on her stomach on top of a bookcase that was next to the crib. She could have rolled onto the floor and been seriously injured. In 1977 I realized that I would have to go back to sea, because I was not earning to my full potential, and I wanted to upgrade my license from Second Mate to Chief Mate. Sally understood and supported me, although it was a difficult thing for her to accept. Kirsten was two years old at the time, and Sally was unaccustomed to long periods of separation. She wondered how she would be able to adjust to the responsibilities of property ownership and raising a child in my absence. I was convinced that she could adjust easily because of her independent nature and flexibility.

OFF TO SEA ONCE AGAIN

After searching for possible positions on board a tanker or freighter, I contacted an oil company, which operated two tankers between several East Coast ports and Nederland, Texas. One was a World War II - vintage T-3 tanker, which had been lengthened by adding a new hull section amidships. The living accommodations were divided between two superstructures, one amidships and one aft. The deck officers lived in the quarters amidships, and the engineers lived in the after section over the engine room. The officer and crew quarters were similar to those of the C-2 Class ships.

I received orders to travel to Nederland, Texas, where the ship was loading chemicals for the East Coast. It was difficult for me to leave, because now a small child had to be factored into the decision along with my wife. I was also feeling somewhat nervous about returning to sea after having been away from the industry for about six years. After the initial paperwork and interviews were completed, I made my way to the dock through strange new surroundings. The entire area was occupied by refineries of all kinds, which were spewing fumes and smoke into the atmosphere. It was hot, and the smell in the air was nauseating.

After stowing my bags in the second mate's room, I changed into my work clothes, not knowing what was ahead, having never sailed on board a tanker before. As I walked out of the deckhouse and looked forward, I noticed the tankerman on cargo watch taking ullage readings in one of the tanks, which were being topped off. ("Ullage" is the remaining unfilled volume of a partially filled tank or container.) It was a calm day, allowing fumes to flow upward from the tank opening and gently drift down toward the deck. The tankerman was standing in the midst of these fumes, which made me wonder what I was getting into.

Topping off is the final stage of loading, in which the product rises to a predetermined level depending upon the specific gravity and temperature of the cargo. In 1977, many ships were still loading with their cargo tanks open to the atmosphere. This method was extremely dangerous to the environment as well as to the personnel involved. A long, T-shaped device with gradations showing inches and feet was used to determine the level of the liquid inside the tanks. When it was necessary to obtain a reading on the cargo, the tankerman held his breath and lowered the long part of the device into the liquid. After a second or two he would withdraw it, note the level of the liquid on the stick, and record that reading. Today, major improvements in the process allow the mate on watch to remain in an air-conditioned control room using automated gauges, the result being physically safer conditions and less air pollution. Many of the cargoes carried were considered the "light ends" of the refining process, and most were carcinogenic— such as xylene, heptane, hexane, toluene, benzene, gasoline, and lube oil.

The cargoes were stowed in tanks divided by steel bulkheads. Piping connected all the tanks and was arranged so that the cargo could be loaded or discharged from either side of the ship. The central part of the ship was divided into smaller tanks, piped so that each tank could be loaded and discharged individually via steam pumps. Much of the equipment on deck was severely rusted and appeared to be in a generally run-down state.

The food was acceptable, but the cleanliness of the galley was not. Often I would enter the pantry, turn on the light, and see small cockroaches scatter across the room. The officers dined at one long table on the starboard side aft. If anyone made a mess at his place, it was noted by the messman. He did not comment on the messy eating habits of the individual, but took more subtle means to make his point. As the officers filed in at the next meal, one place setting would have a paper placemat set in front of the chair. This poor, embarrassed individual would then be subjected to much harassment from his shipmates.

One day while engaged in tank-cleaning operations, part of which involved blowing and venting fumes to the deck, the chief mate and I noticed a crewmember coming toward us smoking a cigarette. The chief mate immediately ordered him from the deck and terminated his employment. Later that day, I met this crewman at the airport, and he seemed very agitated. When I asked him why he was nervous, he replied that he was going to be late for a funeral. I said that it would probably be ok if he was late, and that the family would understand. He said, "Oh no, you don't understand. It's my funeral."

While proceeding along the Florida keys, one beautiful sunny day I was relaxing with a coffee on the starboard bridge wing. I looked down at the water rushing by along the hull of the ship and suddenly found myself looking at the bottom of the sea! Needless to say, I was shocked and rushed into the wheelhouse to obtain a navigation fix of the vessel's position. After plotting the position, it was clear that we were on the course line and all was well. The surprising fact was that the depth of water was over 200 feet deep. I was amazed that the water was so transparent. It did make the adrenalin flow for a short while, though.

On one occasion, Sally and Kirsten met the ship at a remote dock in East Providence, Rhode Island. They toured the ship, had dinner on board, and spent the night, getting up at three o'clock in the morning before the ship sailed. We had to take advantage of every opportunity to see one another in those days. Security was not as tight at the terminals as it is today. My family might not be allowed through the terminal gate today.

NORTH TO ALASKA

After a year on board the chemical tanker, I learned about a company named Arco Marine, Inc., located in Long Beach, California. After spending several months at home with my family, it was time to travel to California and begin the next phase of my career. Upon reporting to the main office, I was instructed to check a recorded telephone message each day. This message contained information regarding the names of company ships due to arrive that day, along with the respective docking times. My duty was to report on board each vessel and observe the loading or discharge operations, thereby becoming familiar with each type of ship. I was very impressed with this company for the thorough way in which new officers were trained prior to boarding company vessels. Marine transportation companies that I had joined in the past were not nearly as willing to go the extra mile for training and indoctrination of new employees.

Arco operated a large fleet of crude oil tankers engaged in the transport of North Slope crude from Valdez, Alaska, to the West Coast of the United States, Panama, and Hawaii. The fleet consisted of several classifications of vessels. I served in the capacity of chief officer on at least one vessel of each classification and second officer on the 55,000-ton ships.

The following table lists the classes according to deadweight tonnage:

NUMBER OF SHIPS	TONNAGE
2	55,000 Tons
2	70,000 Tons
1	90,000 Tons
3	120,000 Tons
2	188,000 Tons
2	265,000 Tons

After large reserves of crude oil were discovered on the North Slope of Alaska, it became necessary to determine the safest and most efficient means to deliver the oil to the "Lower 48." The first concept introduced consisted of retrofitting a tanker called the *Manhattan* with a specialized bow that could ride up on the ice and break its way through by sheer weight. The voyage of the *Manhattan* through northern Canadian waters was unsuccessful due to the large amount of ice, however, and the vessel had to be accompanied by a Canadian icebreaker.

A consortium of several large oil companies then constructed at great expense a pipeline stretching from the Alaskan North Slope to Valdez, a port on the south coast of Alaska. To this day, after the oil is extracted from the ground, it is transported through the pipeline to storage tanks in Valdez, which provide reserve storage capacity in the event that ships are delayed by rough weather. The flow of oil in the pipeline can be slowed but cannot be stopped in extremely cold temperatures, or it might become too thick to pump. During loading, the terminal operator controls the cargo valves by computer from a central control room. These valves regulate the rate of flow of crude oil to the ships as it makes its way by gravity from the storage tanks high on a mountainside.

After the two-week observation period, I was assigned to a vessel called the *Arco Fairbanks* of the 120,000-ton class. I served as second mate on voyages from Valdez to Long Beach from September 1979 to June 1980. The captain was a graduate of

Maine Maritime Academy and very self-assured in his duties and responsibilities. I remember him particularly for several orders that he repeated each time the vessel docked. As soon as the ship was in position and ready to be secured alongside the dock, he would give the command, "Ok. Tie her up front and back and don't forget your fire wire." The fire wire is a wire that was put over the side from the outboard quarter of the ship after docking. It was rigged so that one end is made fast on deck and led through a chock in the rail, with the eye in the other end hanging just above the surface of the water. In case of a fire on the dock, a tug would come alongside, make fast to the wire, and pull the ship off the dock. Another command that stands out in my memory was one he gave each time the tugs were made up alongside and the vessel was prepared to sail: "Ok let her go, ends to the middle." He meant that the ship's crew should take in bow and stern lines first, and then proceed to the midships area and take in the springlines.

Upon completion of a cargo discharge late one cold, snowy night, with the wind blowing thirty to forty knots, the bos'n and I were making our rounds of the decks as the vessel approached the pilot station. Usually the bos'n would walk from the deckhouse to the bow on one side, and I would walk on the other side, checking for anything that was not secured for sea. I noticed that one of the portable electronic cargo-measuring tapes was missing from the holding rack in the pumproom. I will always remember that particular stay in port for the excessive amount of snowfall we received in a 24-hour period. Each tank lid was capped with about 12 inches of snow. I reached out my arm on each tank lid to sweep the snow off, searching for the missing measuring tape, and sure enough, I located the tape at number one starboard. It was fortunate for me that I had found it, because only a few hours later the vessel experienced thirty- to forty-foot waves from dead ahead. If that tape had gone unnoticed, the seas would have washed it overboard—an unhappy thought given the substantial cost of a tape.

One incident, which could have resulted in serious injury to me, happened in the port of Long Beach, California. It involved the operation of docking the Arco Fairbanks alongside a company dock. During docking it was the policy to use two wires and one "poly" line as springs, both fore and aft. A spring is either a line or wire used to hold the ship in position alongside the dock so that it cannot move forward or back. In order to save on labor, the poly line was usually led to the dock first and then two turns were taken on a mooring bitt. This allows the line to slack itself under tension, as the ship moves forward alongside the dock. When the ship is in position the line is already tight and there is no need for the use of a stopper to transfer the line from the winch to the mooring bitt. The bos'n, thinking that the vessel was in position, made up the line securely with several additional turns. I noticed that the line was drawing extremely tight and it appeared to be about to part. I quickly attempted to throw the additional turns off the bitt to prevent the line from parting. This turned out to be a very unwise thing to do. The tension caused the line to snap toward my chest with such force that it knocked me to the deck.

As I lay on the deck, the first thought that came to mind was that I was still conscious and not in bad pain. I picked myself up and was able to continue with the docking process. I reported the incident to the captain and completed the necessary paperwork. A subsequent visit and several x-rays at a nearby doctor's office did not reveal any broken bones. I was, however, bruised in the stomach and chest area and experiencing considerable pain. Some lessons are learned from textbooks and some are learned from first hand experience. This is one that I never forgot. It is clear that I should have cleared the area of personnel and let the line part. Needless to say, it never happened again.

Arco vessels also called at several remote areas in Cook Inlet, where the danger of currents and ice posed serious problems while loading. Cook Inlet is a large body of water, which leads to Anchorage, Alaska. The port of Drift River consists of a steel platform located well offshore. It was necessary for shore personnel to be transported by air to the platform in order to moor the vessel to the dock and conduct loading operations. Once, while loading our vessel, ice built up between the dock and the ship to the point that it became necessary to disconnect the loading arms twice and sail the ship. The ice would clear after the ship was disconnected, which allowed the vessel to return to the dock and resume loading.

Nikiski was another loading port we visited on the eastern shore of Cook Inlet. It was not possible to go ashore from the Drift River platform, but Nikiski was a port on the mainland, which allowed ship personnel to go ashore if desired. On one very rare occasion, I took the opportunity to go to a nearby town to explore the area and do some shopping. While walking along the street, I met a mother and son sitting at the corner of an intersection with a crate containing several Alaskan Husky puppies that they were giving away to anyone who might be interested. I really wanted one of those puppies, but I was sure the captain would not allow one on board. Upon returning to the vessel, I mentioned the puppies to the captain, and much to my surprise he told me that I could have transported a puppy to the "Lower 48" on board the ship. I was disappointed because my chance to have a puppy for free had slipped away. It was not possible for me to return the next day to find the puppy because the ship was due to sail within hours. It would have been a new thing to have a puppy as a shipmate.

LIFE ASHORE

While I was making the transition from a chemical tanker to the Alaskan crude oil trade, we purchased what had originally been a seasonal home near the ocean. It had been upgraded during World War II to a year-round dwelling. When we moved in, brush was growing all through the backyard and right up to the house. Most of it was Japanese knotweed, more commonly known as bamboo, which is fast growing and had taken over the yard. I hired a contractor friend to rip out all of the weeds that he could. He also picked up many large rocks and pushed them across the back boundary to form a fieldstone wall. After many days of work, the yard began to take shape.

Our house was one of two nearly identical dwellings built next to one another by two sisters and sharing a common garage. The property line split the garage in half, giving each sister one half of a two-car garage. When we purchased the property, this meant that we owned one half of the garage and our neighbors owned the other half. It was painted to match the color scheme of our neighbor's house for several years, and then altered to that of our house. After several years, I constructed a petition dividing the two halves internally and mounted wood shelves. We could not keep a vehicle in the garage due to the immense amount of "stuff" that we had already collected. Our half also served as a storage place for the Whirlwind, my first sailboat.

Our second daughter, Katelyn Mary Grimes, was born into this world on June 22, 1982. It was so exciting to prepare a new bedroom *for Katelyn! We could walk out the front door of our house, look to the right, and there was the open ocean. What a place for our two girls to spend their childhood. The scenic walk to town from our front door took only ten minutes. I often carried my Mistral sailboard down the street from the house and launched it at the beach. Sailing from there was a little frustrating because of the frequent light winds encountered in the area. The girls had many birthday parties on Old Garden Beach at the end of the street.*

BACK TO SEA

After one year I received a call from the Arco operations manager with a request that I sail as chief mate on board the *Arco Heritage*. This was a surprise, given that I had only recently acquired my Chief Mate license. I was to board the ship, "let the lines go," and bring her to Boston. Upon arrival, another chief mate would relieve me so that I could return to finish my vacation at home. I signed on, even though I had not been at home with my family for long. Reporting on board, I learned that the ship had docked only a few hours before my arrival. I would have to discharge the ballast and load the vessel prior to sailing.

The *Arco Heritage* and *Arco Prestige* were known as "valve turners." On this type of ship, the tank valves were manually operated wheel valves located on deck. These ships represented the older type of oil tanker with the deckhouses located forward and aft. The deck officers lived in the midship superstructure, and the engineers lived aft, near the engine room.

The captain asked, "Have you ever sailed as chief mate before?" I replied in the negative, but added that I learned quickly and would give this assignment my best effort. He replied, "Great, I fired the last chief mate and now they send me one who has never sailed as mate. What the f...... good are you?" Angered by this exchange, I picked up my bag and headed for the gangway with the intention of returning home. As I turned away from him, I said, "If you don't want me on board, I will return home to my family." He chased after me, saying, "Wait a minute, come back. We will work it out somehow."

The next several days at the dock were very busy as I learned the pipelines and procedures, assisted by the pumpman. As the vessel made its way toward Boston, I did my best to make a good impression each day at sea. After several days, the captain approached me on deck, saying, "You know, I have been watching you for the last several days, and I like what I see. If you stick with me, on the first trip you won't know anything. On the second trip you may start to learn something, and by the third trip you might become a good chief mate. How about it? Do you want to stay with me?"

I replied, "Thank you, Captain, I appreciate the good words, but I am on vacation and was informed that I was required only until the ship arrived in Boston." I was relieved upon arrival in Boston so that I could enjoy the rest of my vacation time, and for the next year I was assigned as second mate even though my performance evaluations were excellent. Finally I asked the president of the company to explain why I had not been assigned as chief officer.

He stated that he was of the impression that I had refused to accept assignments as chief mate. He would not reveal how he might have drawn that conclusion, but it was clear to me that the problem had been caused by my refusal to accept the offer of the captain of the *Arco Heritage* one year before. I made it known that I was ready to start working as chief mate, and I worked in that capacity until resigning from the company in 1990. It was a lesson for me in how far people will go to twist a situation to suit their ends, regardless of the consequences to someone else. That experience taught me to speak up for myself if I feel that I have been wronged. Following my tours on the old valve turners, I worked as chief mate on most of the other classes of ships.

One captain was so particular in his conduct of business on board that hardly any of the chief mates in the company would sail with him. I kept being reassigned to his ship and could not understand why he appeared to like me so much. Every time that he suggested a project should be done "when you get a chance," it meant right away. I would immediately assign several of the deck crew to the project. I did not question his orders as some of the other chief mates did, so we got along just fine.

The pumpman on the *Arco Fairbanks* was a fine and competent shipmate who helped me whenever I needed assistance. Each night in port, after the nightly news, whether the ship was loading or discharging, he left the control room at 2330 in order to listen to Johnny Carson's monologue. We humored him because he was the best pumpman in the company and we did not want to lose him from the crew. Another interesting custom that he observed daily was to open the door to his room and play his favorite song, "Take This Job and Shove It," sung by Johnny Paycheck. His room was two doors down the passageway from the officers' dining room, so we became very familiar with the lyrics of that song—"Take this job and shove it / I ain't working here no more."

Cargo operations were conducted from a centrally located control room, usually on the main deck. The chief mate and pumpman were responsible for supervising cargo operations. The engineering department maintained the inert gas system, propulsion equipment, and all systems that were essential for everyday operation of the vessel. The deckhands assisted with cargo measurement, valves, and other duties necessary to facilitate operations.

Most control rooms are similar, with minor variations. Normally, the gauges and controls are displayed at eye level so that the chief mate and pumpman can view them easily. The cargo tank valves are hydraulically actuated using toggle switches on the slanted control console. A schematic diagram on one side shows the respective locations of pipelines and valves in the tanks. The chief mate actuates the cargo tank valves while maintaining radio contact with a crewmember stationed at the appropriate remote-control panel on deck. The other side of the cargo console shows the location of the pumproom valves. The pumpman and the chief officer, along with the other watch-standing mates, supervise the loading and discharging of cargo and ballast.

A SAFETY PROBLEM IS SOLVED

D uring the latter part of the twentieth century, many tankers were mysteriously exploding while at sea in ballast condition (i.e., without cargo). The cause of these explosions was the subject of prolonged scientific and engineering investigations. After many months, a common thread was found linking the majority of the explosions.

At the time of its catastrophe, each vessel had been engaged in tank-cleaning operations, which consisted of pumping water into the cargo tanks under high pressure. Scientists concluded that the high-pressure spray passing into the atmosphere of the tank caused a static electric charge, and when the spray passed steel objects in the tank, sparks were created, not unlike small bolts of lightning. The result was predictable when one thinks of the "fire triangle" method of explaining how combustion occurs. A fire requires three elements: fuel, oxygen, and a source of ignition. The tank atmosphere at the completion of cargo discharge was a mixture of hydrocarbon fumes and air that had been drawn into the tank, and these provided the first two elements. Only one more thing was needed to complete the triangle. The static spark was the missing link, resulting in a catastrophic event.

The solution was to design a system that could replace the air with a non-explosive gas, thereby eliminating one leg of the fire triangle. The exhaust gases formed as a result of combustion in the ship's boilers contained large percentages of nitrogen, moisture, and soot, and engineers concluded that if the exhaust could be voided of soot and water, mainly nitrogen would remain. The cargo tank openings, known as ullage caps, were sealed, and a system was designed that allowed the cleansed exhaust gases to be pumped into the cargo tanks. A device known as a "scrubber" removed the soot, and the system was set up to allow the engineering department to monitor the gas, ensuring that the oxygen content did not exceed 5% by volume. As long as the oxygen remained below 7% by volume, combustion could not occur, so this system incorporated a safety factor of approximately 2%. Gauges were fitted in the cargo control room enabling the mate on watch to monitor the percentage of oxygen in the cargo tanks. If the percentage rose above 5%, the engine room was notified and the necessary adjustments were made.

Upon completion of discharge, the tank atmosphere was non-explosive due to its low oxygen content, but another factor had to be considered in order to ensure the safety of the ship and its crew. If the ship collided with another vessel or object and the hull was breached, air would suddenly enter the tanks, and the collision would very likely cause a spark, thereby completing the fire triangle. The result would most likely be a catastrophic event. It followed that a method had to be devised whereby the hydrocarbon fumes left inside the tanks could be purged immediately upon departure of the vessel from port. The solution was to use the pipe system that was already in place to transport exhaust gases to the tanks. Each tank is equipped with a vertical pipe, the bottom of which is open at a height of about eighteen inches above the tank floor. The top end is fitted with a hinged cap, which can be opened to allow gases to escape.

The chief mate is responsible for ensuring that each cargo tank is purged as soon as possible following the ship's departure. A schedule is drawn up that specifies how long each tank is to be purged. The inert gas system is started, and the caps on each purge pipe are opened one pair at a time. The gas enters the top of the tank, forming a layer within the tank atmosphere, and as this layer of gas builds downward into the tank, the hydrocarbon fumes are forced upward through the respective purge pipe. Each tank is purged for two to three hours, depending upon its volume. When the mate on watch is relieved, he changes the purge pipes in accordance with the written schedule. One glance from the bridge will allow the mate on watch to determine when a tank has been successfully purged. The clear hydrocarbon fumes change to a smoky appearance. The tank is tested at this point with a device known as a tank-scope. No hydrocarbon fumes should remain in the tank.

A SEAGOING SWIMMING POOL

L ife on board in the tropics can be hot, with little relief, especially if you are an engineer working in the engine room for eight hours a day. The engineers of the *Arco Prudhoe Bay* decided to solve this issue by fabricating a makeshift swimming pool on deck below the starboard bridge wing. They gathered the necessary number of steel plates and angle iron and welded up a square box approximately 6 feet high and about 25 feet on each side. Apparently, little consideration was given to stress calculations, because the walls were of the same thickness and strength both high and low. The ship's fire main system was used to fill the pool with seawater each morning, and it was emptied late in the evening. No consideration was given to the possibility of algae, bacteria, or human diseases being present, nor was any provision provided for filtering the water from the sea.

When the makeshift pool was filled for the first time, the sides collapsed outward, spilling all the water and the several crewmembers relaxing inside across the deck. I was not fortunate enough to be on board to witness what must have been a very amusing sight. It was later constructed with more bracing around the bottom. I must say that on the few trips that I made to the Panama Canal, it felt very relaxing and therapeutic to soak in the relatively cool water under the moonlight after a long, hot bridge watch. Unfortunately, the pool did not last long once the company authorities learned of it. We were ordered to disassemble it and stow the parts for their proper use at a later time.

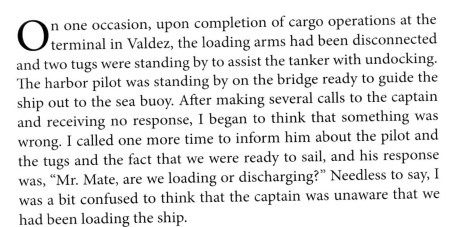

ARE WE LOADING OR DISCHARGING?

On one occasion, upon completion of cargo operations at the terminal in Valdez, the loading arms had been disconnected and two tugs were standing by to assist the tanker with undocking. The harbor pilot was standing by on the bridge ready to guide the ship out to the sea buoy. After making several calls to the captain and receiving no response, I began to think that something was wrong. I called one more time to inform him about the pilot and the tugs and the fact that we were ready to sail, and his response was, "Mr. Mate, are we loading or discharging?" Needless to say, I was a bit confused to think that the captain was unaware that we had been loading the ship.

I proceeded forward to my normal undocking station on the bow, made up the assist tug, and prepared to let the lines go. When I notified the captain that we were ready to let go, he replied "Ok, Mr. Mate, single up on your springs and double up on your breasts." Needless to say, we got a laugh out of that comment and commenced letting the lines go.

It has been the custom since the days of sail that the chief mate is in charge of the forward area of the ship, including the anchors. Heaving and letting go the anchor on a large sailing vessel was an involved process requiring someone well qualified to supervise. This custom has been carried down through the ages, even though all officers and most crewmembers are well versed in matters pertaining to anchoring procedures. The third mate assists with relaying commands and keeps the logbooks on the bridge, while the second mate assists on the stern.

THE SHIPYARD CLEANUP

Merchant vessels of all types are required to undergo periodic overhauls and inspections in order to satisfy United States Coast Guard and classification society standards. The process required to prepare a tanker for overhaul is more complex than that for a general cargo ship. The tanker must be certified as gas-free by a qualified marine chemist prior to the commencement of any repair work. This means that all cargo piping and cargo tanks must be free of oil fumes or residues of past cargo. All void spaces, including but not limited to cofferdams, ballast tanks, machinery spaces, and storage lockers, must be free of fumes.

In my opinion, the shipyard cleanup is probably the most difficult and challenging aspect of the chief mate's job. The first time I was faced with this daunting task, I was sunbathing on deck after having sailed from the discharge port in Panama when a deckhand approached to inform me that the captain wished to see me. As I entered the captain's office, he asked if I had done a shipyard cleanup before, and I replied that I had not. He stated that we had about one week to prepare the ship for the shipyard. Not knowing where to begin, I gathered all the deck crew in the mess room in order to explain the operation, which lay ahead and the fact that I needed all the help possible. I made it clear that the process was new to me and that I would need the assistance of all hands. I was aware that many of the crew were familiar with the process and that I could benefit greatly from their knowledge and experience. It went well, and I was commended for the efficient way in which it was handled.

The process is most always performed at sea consuming a week or more with all hands working together as a team. Following the completion of cargo discharge and immediately after the ship has sailed, all tanks are purged in accordance with the chief mate's predetermined schedule. The tanks are then washed in several stages, using seawater under high pressure. The water is delivered through the cargo piping to programmable machines on deck and then to nozzles positioned approximately 12 to 20 feet below the deck.

The tank washings are sucked from the tank by means of an eductor, which is connected to the bottom piping. The eductor is actuated by water being pumped into one end of the bottom piping and discharged through the other, larger-diameter end, which creates a partial vacuum. The middle of the eductor is connected to the cargo piping, allowing access to all cargo tanks. There are three slop tanks designed to receive the tank washings, and these are piped together so as to allow as much water as possible to separate from the oil. After each tank has been water washed, it is well ventilated using portable air blowers. In the last step in the process, called "mucking the tank," men enter the tank and scrape the remaining sludge and residues from the floor. In those years it was permissible to discard the residues overboard a certain distance from the coast.

The final step in the cleanup process is called the line flush. Water is taken in from the sea and pumped through the bottom pipelines and risers to the deck. Each branch line is then flushed to the manifold connections at the ship's rail. The manifold valves are in the open position, with an extension fitted so that water exiting the manifold will flow to the rail and then overboard. This procedure allows ship personnel to visually monitor the discharge as it flows over the side. (This operation is no longer allowed at sea.) During one of these line flushes, the captain instructed me to pressurize all three bottom pipelines simultaneously and equally.

I followed his instructions and did not observe any oil residues in the water being flushed. I notified the captain that the flush was completed and that we were ready to dock at the shipyard the next day.

That night as I lay in my bunk, I visualized the water flowing forward from the pumproom through the three cargo lines and then over the side. All of a sudden I realized that one essential piece of the process had been omitted. The three bottom lines were numbered from one to three with number one on the starboard side, number two in the center, and number three on the port side. The number one and three lines were connected in number one center cargo tank, and I realized that the valve in the middle of number one center tank, which connected the number one and three lines, had been closed during the line flush. It was clear to me that no water could have passed through the section of pipe in number one center tank. I informed the captain the next morning that it would be advisable to do one more line flush prior to entering port. I suggested that water be pumped forward through number one line, across number one center tank, and through the crossover valve. It would then flow through number three aft to the riser. Clean water began flowing from the manifold, but after several minutes it changed to a brownish color, and shortly after that it turned to black. A few seconds later it cleared again, but that was enough time to show me to that we'd made the right decision. The captain said that it was a good thing we had done the final line flush, and of course I agreed.

THE BENEFITS OF GOOD COMMUNICATION

Good communication is essential for an efficiently managed vessel. The first shipyard cleanup that I performed was an excellent example of this principle. Prior to beginning the operation I had no first hand knowledge of the procedures involved and of the problems that could develop. I decided to take advantage of the knowledge and experience that many of the crew had regarding this type of operation. I called a meeting of the entire deck crew to discuss the cleanup and it turned out to be the best move I could have made. I presented the task which lay ahead and made it clear to all present that I welcomed any suggestions as to ways in which the operation could be done better. The ship arrived at the shipyard and the marine chemist certified her to be gas free. This cleanup could not have gone any better and all hands were commended for their hard work and assistance.

When I was a cadet at Maine Maritime Academy, I repeatedly heard the phrase, "familiarity breeds contempt." It was the general feeling at the time that if the officers and crew on board ships became too familiar with one another, the crew would attempt to take advantage of the officer. This attitude is counter-productive and results in a poorly run operation. Several years after the cleanup mentioned above, while attending Maine Maritime Academy Graduate School, I was asked to write a paper about one experience that would exemplify the importance of good communications on board ship. I chose the shipyard cleanup as the topic for my paper and received an A+ grade.

This principle was demonstrated again later in my career when I began working on tugboat decks. Everyone works together on a tug, with little or no distinction between crewmembers with regard to position or license. The crew often jokes with the officers and vice versa, which serves to pass the time in a more relaxed fashion. By contrast, I was once told to leave the crew messroom when I was chief mate on board a ship because "It wasn't my side."

Unfortunately, communication can be used to make one person appear to know more at the expense of another. While serving as chief officer on board one of the tankers, this fact was demonstrated on several occasions. If the second officer had observed me omitting something on deck or making an obvious mistake he would wait until all of the officers were seated at the same table at lunch or dinner. He then would ask me why I did something the way I had in order to purposely embarrass me. After several of these exchanges I made it clear to the second officer that if he had a comment to make regarding the way that I did things, I would prefer that he tell me in private. This is something that a very insecure person would do, and I am certain that this type of interpersonal interchange occurs in any occupation, not just on board ship.

INSPECTING THE DOUBLE BOTTOMS

The *Arco Alaska* and *Arco California* each carried approximately 1.8 million barrels of crude oil. In addition to the *Arco Texas*, these two ships had flush main decks, meaning that the main deck was one unbroken surface. They were considered "ahead of their time," having been designed with double bottom tanks. One extremely important requirement of the Oil Pollution Act of 1990 is that tankers and barges used to transport petroleum products be constructed with double bottom tanks by the year 2015. These double bottom tanks must extend completely to the upper freeboard deck. This requirement provides a void space of about 12 feet, which separates the oil in the cargo tanks from the seawater outside the hull. When an oil tanker is fully laden with cargo, the double bottom tanks are empty. Most of the hull's longitudinal and transverse framing is located in the double bottom tanks. Above these otherwise void spaces, the center cargo tanks are essentially huge boxes with flat bottoms and sides. The port and starboard cargo tanks are flat on the bottom with exposed frames lining the sides. The main 16-inch-diameter cargo pipelines passed from aft to forward inside the center cargo tanks, above the tank floors.

Although the *Arco Alaska* and *Arco California* were constructed with double bottom tanks from skin to skin, they did not fulfill the new requirements entirely. Their double bottom tanks extended from one side of the hull to the other under the cargo tanks, but not to the main deck. It was essential that only two double bottom tanks be opened at one time while the vessel was conducting cargo operations. If a list developed due to uneven levels in the cargo tanks, it would be increased to a large degree by the water in the double bottom tanks flowing to the lower side of the ship. This condition, known as Free Surface Effect, is the negative effect that water has on the stability of a ship when it is unobstructed and allowed to flow freely. Imagine two ice cube trays, one with internal separations and one without. Fill them both with water and carry them from one end of the room to the other. Which one will be easier to keep level? Try it, and the result will become obvious.

It was the duty of the chief officer to inspect the double bottom tanks, most always when the cargo tanks were full. It was hard not to be overwhelmed by the thought of having 75 feet of crude oil pressing downward above my head as I felt my way through small access holes with several flashlights, a breathing apparatus, and various assorted meters for monitoring the tank atmosphere. I mustn't forget the handy-talkie radio used for communication. It was necessary to climb down a ladder through the various levels with all of the above-mentioned gear hanging on my person. The purpose of these inspections was to locate any cracks in the steel bulkheads that lined the cargo tanks.

ARCO SPIRIT AND *ARCO INDEPENDENCE*

The *Arco Spirit* and *Arco Independence* were 1,100 feet long, with cargo capacities of 2,400,000 barrels. They were utilized between Valdez, Alaska and an oil storage terminal at Charco Azul, near the town of Puerto Armuelles, on the west coast of Panama. The oil was stored there temporarily, to be transferred via pipeline to the Atlantic side of the Isthmus of Panama, from whence it was loaded on board ships bound for various world ports and the Gulf of Mexico. Chief mates liked this run because of the long sea passages. There were fewer port calls, which translated into less work and stress for the chief mate.

These ships were more difficult to work, however, due to their size and tonnage. I had to plan ahead if I was going forward to handle lines or perform repairs on deck. There was a bicycle on board with a wire basket for carrying tools and parts. One lesson I learned soon after reporting on board for the first time was to take an ample number of batteries for the portable handheld VHF radio, especially in cold weather. It was embarrassing when the captain called on one occasion with important information and I was left standing on the bow unable to respond. The tank-cleaning machines were portable but very heavy and difficult to move around the deck. I supervised one shipyard cleanup on the *Arco Spirit,* that was extremely challenging. A great deal more planning was necessary in order to minimize the deck crew's labor when moving the machines from tank to tank.

One unique characteristic of the pumproom on the *Arco Spirit* was the elevator. In order to get to the lower level of the pumproom, it is normally necessary on a large tanker to descend half-dozen levels via metal ladders and intermediate platforms. This elevator was constructed with a wire-grated sliding door, which allowed the rider to view the depths of the pumproom on the way up or down. It was quite a sensation to stand inside the elevator while the vessel rolled from side to side, wondering if it would break down at any time. I always took a portable radio with me, because it was not uncommon for the elevator to stop without notice.

It is an amazing fact that these vessels were loaded to a draft of 57 feet of water and could have been loaded even deeper if the channel had been able to accommodate such a draft.

A SHIP IS RECYCLED

During the 1970s, a 70,000 ton, oil tanker exploded and burned in Texas and was declared a total loss. Arco Marine purchased the remains of the vessel and salvaged the portion of the hull extending from the bulkhead separating the cofferdam and the pumproom to the stern. A new forward section making up the cargo tanks was fabricated and welded to the salvaged stern section.

The new ship was designed and built to the maximum length and beam that could transit the lock system of the Panama Canal. She was strange in appearance, and the crews who operated her were quick to give her various nicknames. She made two voyages from the Pacific Ocean to the Gulf of Mexico, after which she worked between Valdez and various West Coast ports.

The crew's quarters, which were aft on the port and starboard sides, contained the original portholes. Some changes had become necessary when the ship was redesigned, however, due to stability requirements. In order to provide additional buoyancy and freeboard aft, the area outside the crew staterooms was closed in, thereby blocking the view from inside the rooms. It seemed strange to gaze out the portholes only to see solid white steel. One creative deckhand painted a nautical scene on the steel to improve the view from his room.

The captain was easily excited when confronted with frustrating situations. He had apparently experienced difficulties with government authorities on a previous vessel, which had resulted in a fine, and as a result he had developed a strong dislike of government intervention of any kind. Occasionally at dinner, one of the deck officers might offer the comment, "Oh, by the way, Captain, I heard that the vessel will be boarded for inspection tomorrow." This would agitate him to the point where he would rage about how much he disliked shoreside authority of any kind.

On one occasion, it was necessary to ventilate a cargo tank so that I could enter and test a valve that was suspected of leaking. After testing the tank atmosphere, I entered the tank, observing all safety procedures. I called the third mate by radio and asked him to put considerable head pressure on the cargo line to test the valve. As I was standing on the floor of the center tank, next to the sump, which contained the main and stripping suction valves I heard a tremendous noise resembling the sound of a train approaching. Then a wave of water erupted from the sump and crept rapidly across the tank bottom. I made it to the ladder leading to the next level before the water reached me. As soon as I was certain that I was out of harm's way, I called the Third Officer and told him to close the valves leading into the tank. He did not understand that I only wanted the water to pressurize the closed tank valve. I got a first hand look at what it is like when a tank valve is opened under pressure, even though it was not planned. The Third Officer and I had a rather heated debriefing following the incident. I don't believe he will forget that day.

Detecting no indication of a problem, I exited the tank. As I climbed out of the tank top, I met the captain and informed him that the valve in question was functioning normally. He replied, "It is a mystery of the sea. Close the tank; we are done." I was relieved to know that I would not have to pursue the matter further. On such occasions he demonstrated a tendency to be casual and low key, but on other occasions he would go in the opposite direction and fly off the handle.

One incident stands out in my memory regarding a shipyard cleanup done on board this particular vessel. While going through the mucking stage of the cleanup the crew encountered a difficult area where, due to the construction of the tank and the shape of the hull, it was extremely difficult to reach much of the accumulated sediment on the ledges and other surfaces. The captain decided that the way to attack this problem was to use water pressure from fire hoses to wash the sediment into the bottom areas of the tank. I took the necessary precautions regarding testing and ventilation and entered with the crew. It was difficult to work with the hydrocarbon testing equipment on my person so I set the meter on a nearby ledge. We went about the cleanup process, but I began to feel somewhat light headed. I observed the "pretty rainbow color" of water and oily mixture being sucked into the stripping valve. It was apparent to me that something was amiss. I reached for the meter and the battery had gone dead. It was then clear that the atmosphere was becoming dangerous because of the fumes being released as the muck was being broken up. I ordered everyone out of the tank immediately. It was one of those lessons that we can learn from, which did not result in personal injury or damage to property.

I had a difference of opinion with a female room steward, which resulted in a slight argument and hard feelings between us. I am not sure of the cause of the disagreement, but what transpired after that is worthy of note. She finished cleaning my room, and I went about my duties throughout the day. That night when I turned in and began to doze off, my skin felt irritated and began to itch. I turned on the light and examined the sheets. I had to chuckle at my discovery, even though I was feeling angry at the same time. The room steward had apparently sprinkled salt crystals between the sheets to make a point. What that point was, I am not certain, but I never bothered her again. The next day when she entered my room, we smiled at one another and wished each other well.

LOOSE BUTTERWORTH PLATE

On one trip the crew of the *Arco Sag River* had finished washing the clean ballast tanks on the day before entering Valdez. The segregated clean ballast tanks are fitted with access fittings in the deck, known as butterworth plates, which allow vessel personnel to lower portable cleaning machines and associated gear into the tanks. Long-handled T-shaped wrenches are used to turn the wedge-shaped devices known as "dogs" that secure the plates in place. At the end of the day I instructed the deck crew to check the plates in order to ascertain that they had been secured. I was busy and did not follow behind them to ensure that the checks had been made. On the following day the vessel entered port and commenced loading, upon completion of which we sailed for Long Beach, California. When I assumed the watch at 0400 on the morning after departure, I immediately noticed that the ship was rolling more to port than starboard during each successive roll. The ship was developing a port list, and I set out to determine the cause of the problem. After being relieved from the watch at 0800, I went to the cargo control room to check the levels of all ballast and cargo tanks. The cause of the list was obvious as soon as I checked the two clean ballast tanks. There was about twenty feet of seawater in the number three, port ballast tank. I determined that the crew had not properly secured one of the port plates at the completion of cleaning operations on the previous day. The seas had built up to eight to ten feet in height, causing green water to wash over the decks. On each roll, as the water rushed across the deck, a portion of it flowed into number three port ballast tank.

After entering the tonnages into the computer, it was clear that the vessel was experiencing stresses that were close to exceeding the maximum allowable limit. I instructed the pumpman to start the clean ballast pump immediately. Over the next several hours we successfully pumped the water overboard. A serious incident could have occurred as a result of the neglect of ship personnel to follow orders. I usually double check almost everything done on deck, but this one time when I did not could have had very serious consequences.

SALLY'S VOYAGE

Sally joined me aboard the *Arco Sag River* in Cherry Point, Washington, in order to experience life on board an Alaskan crude oil tanker. Our first port of call was Valdez, Alaska, where part of the cargo of crude oil was to be loaded. From there, the vessel proceeded to Drift River, Alaska, to top off all cargo tanks. Upon the completion of loading, we sailed for Long Beach, California, where we were to disembark. It did not take long for Sally to become familiar with the ship, the officers, and most of the crew.

Prior to our departure from Cherry Point, several of the cargo tanks were partially loaded with salt water in order to settle the ship's hull deeper in the ocean. This minimizes the degree of rolling and reduces the severity of impacts when a hull encounters heavy seas. Ballast carried in the cargo tanks is considered "dirty" because it is contaminated with the residual oil left over in the tanks after cargo has been discharged. The dirty ballast in the *Arco Sag River* would be discharged to the shore facility in Valdez prior to loading the next cargo.

Two tanks amidships on the *Arco Sag River*, known as segregated ballast tanks (or "clean ballast tanks," as we have just seen), were separate from the cargo system. The ballast carried in these tanks was clean seawater and would be discharged back to sea prior to docking, while the vessel proceeded inbound through Prince William Sound.

The voyage to Valdez was uneventful with the exception of one day of rough weather, which caused the ship to roll during the night. At one point as we both were rolling into each other in bed, Sally asked me if we were all right. I replied, "I think so," in a joking fashion. Needless to say, this upset her for a short time until I reassured her that I had been joking and that all was well. This was the summer of 1981, and Kirsten was six years old on July 24 of that year. Sally had left Kirsten with her grandmother and granddad in Park Forest, Illinois, and then had continued on to Seattle by air. Like any good mother, Sally was apprehensive because Kirsten was so far away, and she feared that something would happen to us, leaving Kirsten alone.

Upon our approach to the dock at the Alyeska Terminal, the fog was so thick that I had to relay distances on the radio to aid in guiding the captain and pilot. The personnel on the bow could see the pier, but those in the wheelhouse were unable to see anything. Sally informed me that she wanted to go ashore and tour Valdez, but I told her that I could not accompany her, so she went with the first assistant engineer. I would not have been able to respond to an emergency on board while loading if I had been on the other side of the harbor. She had been counting on having Alaskan king crab while ashore, but when she returned she said that there was none to be had.

The fog persisted throughout our stay in Valdez, preventing Sally from experiencing the breathtaking scenery. After sailing from there, we had an overnight trip to Cook Inlet, named after the European explorer Captain James Cook, who first voyaged in this area in 1778. A pilot boarded at Homer in preparation for the transit to the Drift River Platform. He joked with Sally by referring to Drift River as "the Riviera of the North," when in reality it is a three-legged steel platform that serves as a mooring location for tankers to dock while loading cargoes of crude oil. The oil is pumped through a pipeline from shore to the vessel, and the line handlers and platform personnel are flown to the platform by helicopter prior to the docking.

Upon completion of loading at Drift River, the ship proceeded to Long Beach, California, where Sally and I were scheduled to disembark. Sally told me that she wanted to be on the bow with me when we anchored in Long Beach. I warned her that she might not really want to do that for reasons of safety, but she insisted on it. When I told her to bring safety glasses, however, I think she began to have second thoughts. When the time came, we prepared to lower the starboard anchor, and a few minutes later we received orders from the bridge to let it go. When we released the brake allowing the anchor to drop into the sea from the hawsepipe, Sally was shocked. Rust, mud, scale, and other debris flew out of the chain locker along with the chain as she cowered to one side behind a ventilator. I am sure she wished she were somewhere else.

We had arranged to meet a friend of Sally while we were in Long Beach, one of the girls who had accompanied Sally to Rockport during the "Super Summer of 70." The friend and her husband rode to the anchorage in a launch and toured the ship on the day that I was relieved to go on vacation. We left the vessel the next day and went to their home in Los Angeles for a visit of several days following which we returned home to Rockport so that I could enjoy my long-awaited time off.

FINAL DAYS OF THE *SAG RIVER*

When ships become obsolete, they are usually dismantled and the remains are sold for scrap. The ships are stripped of any valuable items that can be reused. All cargo and ballast tanks, as well as any other void spaces, are emptied, and the crew is sometimes ordered to deliver the vessel to a "bone yard," which is often in Bangladesh or India. The ship is navigated under its own power onto a sandy beach when the tide is at its highest, and local workers arrive with their torches to begin the process of dismantling the ship. The workers are known as "ship breakers," and the object of their difficult and dangerous work is to salvage all recyclable items, such as office furniture, bedding, and any other items that may be reused. The road running along the beach is lined on both sides with stores selling the salvaged materials.

As I was reading about the beaching process recently, my attention was drawn to a passage describing the author's walk through the remains of a partially scrapped tanker. As he is passing through the officer's living quarters he observes marks on the deck indicating the location of some of the partitions that had separated the rooms. He looks down and discovers several old 1972 editions of the *Baltimore Sun*. I immediately realized that this was a clue to the identity of the vessel in question. His walk then takes him to the bridge wing, where he stops and turns to look toward the outside of the wheelhouse. The ship's name board is still readable, and the name is *Sag River*. It was my old ship, on which I had sailed for approximately one and a half years.

Sally was in the kitchen preparing dinner when I called to her excitedly with the news that our ship was mentioned in the book. I had mixed feelings about my discovery. This ship had been my home away from home for three-month increments and represented a large part of my career. It is always a sad sight to see a ship ending its useful life, but it's especially sad when the ship in question is one upon which you have served. It becomes even sadder when I consider that all the vessels mentioned in this memoir have met a similar fate.

POLLUTION INCIDENTS

It is known by experts in accident forensics that a major incident is most probably the result of several minor incidents or errors occurring simultaneously. If just one of these minor errors had not occurred, the chain of events leading to the major incident would likely be broken. Unfortunately this principle—which is as true of airplane crashes, mountain climbing fatalities, and other disasters as it is of merchant shipping accidents—was made clear to me the hard way in Valdez on a snowy, cold January night.

As painful as it is to relate this incident, I feel that others who may be entering the industry can benefit from my experience. The following paragraphs describe several normal shipboard practices and will show how an omission in any of these practices can cause much embarrassment and emotional stress.

The cargo loading arms are routinely drained of remaining oil upon completion of loading. This is usually accomplished by means of a small drain connection on the bottom of each chiksan, or loading arm. This valve, when opened, allows oil to be drained by gravity directly into the cargo tank through a fitting in the deck. In extremely cold weather, it is possible for residual seawater to have collected in this drain line following the completion of the ballast discharge. This will result in plugging the drain line, thereby preventing any possibility of liquid passing through. The usual practice was to open the drain line valve shortly after the commencement of loading to allow hot cargo to flow into the line, thus melting any ice that had formed. The atmospheric temperature was near zero degrees Fahrenheit throughout cargo operations on the night in question. No one in the deck department remembered to execute this procedure, either because of fatigue or some other unknown reason.

The mast riser valve was left in the open position while draining the loading arms in order to allow gases to escape from the cargo system. Upon completion of loading, the distance from the surface of the oil to the deck was about 4 feet 6 inches, and the temperature of the cargo was approximately 100 degrees Fahrenheit. Large amounts of vapor escape when the cargo is hot, and these vapors expand in a confined space, thereby increasing pressure within the tank. On this night I closed the mast riser valve when I left the cargo control room and rushed out on deck to begin disconnecting the loading arms. As a consequence the internal pressure in the tanks began to increase. This, and the fact that the loading-arm drain lines were plugged with ice, made my attempt to drain the arms unsuccessful.

When I informed the captain of this, he ordered me to use the manual drain valves, and then suggested that I drain the drip pans into the cargo tanks through the Butterworth plates. I turned toward the deckhand as he loosened the plate with a long-handled wrench, and at that point the pressure from the expanding gases inside the tank caused the plate to rise approximately 3 feet from the deck. The black oil on the cargo surface was atomized into a fine spray and blown straight into the air. The wind was blowing from the northwest at about twenty knots, and as the spray rose, it was blown toward the white superstructure of the ship. I saw what had happened and thought that my career had ended right there.

The United States Coast Guard and Alaskan environmental authorities were notified and arrived on scene within a very short time. By this time, the cleanup operations were in progress. It wasn't possible to determine the extent to which oil had gone into Valdez Harbor. The Coast Guard concluded that none had gone into the water, and though this seemed impossible due to the wind,

I was not about to dispute it.

The cleanup was completed in four or five hours despite the snow and ice all over the deck, the twenty-knot wind, and near-zero temperatures. The captain told me to go to bed and that we would talk about it in the morning. This all could have been prevented if the drain had been cleared prior to loading and if I had not closed the mast riser. The seas were rough the next morning, and most of the oil had washed off by the time I awoke. I went to see the captain, and he said in jest, "Did we have a spill last night?" I replied, "Yes Captain, we did," and waited to see if I was to lose my job. He said that I should consider this my "freebee," but that "if it happens again, you will be fired."

On a sunny Sunday afternoon in Long Beach, California, the ship was completing the cargo discharge. One essential aspect of finishing that operation was making certain that the pipelines, which run straight up from the pumproom to the main deck, had been thoroughly drained. The next part of the operation was to gravitate dirty ballast into the aftermost empty cargo tank. Apparently some oil was still in a portion of the line at a point close to the deck.

The accepted procedure for taking dirty ballast was to open the sea chest valves one side at a time, thereby allowing seawater to gravitate into the aftermost tank. As the pumpman started to open the sea chest valve, I noticed that one of the pumproom riser valves was partially open. I activated the control to close it, but it was too late. A small shot of black oil squirted out of the sea chest, and I knew that I was in for a world of trouble. The Coast Guard estimated that about 40 gallons had entered the water. The ship's crew cleaned it thoroughly, and I received a warning for not being more vigilant.

DEATH AT SEA

As I was preparing to leave the *Arco California* for a long-awaited vacation, I spoke with a young fellow who had just joined the vessel for a tour of duty as third officer. He was twenty-one years old and due to be married as soon as his tour ended. After a brief conversation at the gangway, we wished each other well and I departed for the airport. A few weeks after arriving home, I received a telephone call from a company representative who said that he had a request of me. He asked if I would represent the company at a funeral ceremony for the shipmate mentioned above. I was shocked and dismayed at the suddenness of this and did not know quite what to say.

The caller went on to explain that the vessel had been en route to Valdez when the incident took place. The third mate was on watch in the wheelhouse between 0800 and 1200 while some crewmembers were working in the forepeak tank. He apparently was curious as to what they had been doing during the morning, and when everyone broke for lunch, he decided to go forward to check out the work in the tank. Without informing anyone of his intentions, he descended into the forepeak ballast tank. The details of the incident were sketchy, but it was surmised that he had been walking across one of the upper decks and fell from that level into the lower hold. Because one of the cardinal rules of tank entry had been breached, no one else in the crew was aware that he had entered the tank. It is standard procedure that whenever anyone is inside a tank, a safety-watch person will stand by with a radio on deck.

Because this had not been done, no one was aware that he had fallen to the bottom of the tank. His body was not discovered until the work crew returned to the site following lunch. In all likelihood he had died instantly. I will not forget the feeling of grief and sadness when I faced his mother and fiancée at the funeral. All of the family members pleaded with me to offer an explanation, but I could not provide one at the time. I knew only that I was to express my condolences on behalf of the company for his untimely death. It was a stark reminder of the seriousness of adhering to proper safety procedures and of how quickly tragedy can strike when you least expect it.

MAINE MARITIME ACADEMY
MASTER'S DEGREE

In 1989 I decided to apply for a Master's Degree in Maritime Management at Maine Maritime Academy. I reasoned that this was a way to make the transition from seagoing employment to a management position ashore with a major shipping company. Maine Maritime Academy was offering a program that allowed seagoing personnel to attend classes in modular courses while they continued employment at sea. In one month, a student can take two courses covering as much material as is normally covered in a semester. I enrolled, intending to complete the requirements over a period of three years. During the last module, Sally, Kirsten, and Katelyn joined me in Castine for the summer. We rented a house so that we would be together and could enjoy a summer by the sea.

I graduated in 1992 and was awarded a Master's Degree. Before the commencement ceremony, the Assistant Professor of Navigation approached me and said, "I am not going to let you leave here without offering you a full-time position as Assistant Professor of Marine Transportation. Are you interested?" I was excited at the thought of teaching navigation at my alma mater, but after considering all aspects of life in a small rural town, I refused the offer. After graduation, I resigned from Arco Marine so that I could utilize my newly acquired degree in marine management with a marine shipping company. After further investigation, it became obvious that I would have to move away from the Cape

Ann area. Employment opportunities in the port of Boston were scarce, and I did not want to move away from Rockport. This decision meant that it was time to look for a local position once again.

CRUISE BOAT CAPTAIN

While networking for a temporary position locally, I discovered a company that operated a number of small Boston Harbor excursion boats. There were three boats, each capable of carrying 200 to 300 passengers. A relief captain was required so that each full-time captain could have one day off per week. The initial interview was brief, followed by a short excursion upon the waters of operation. The operations manager accompanied me in order to ascertain my ability to handle the boats in their fleet and to familiarize me with Boston Harbor.

On Fridays I operated a ferry to one of the harbor islands, followed by two half-hour lunch boat cruises. It was often necessary to make an additional trip to the island in the afternoon, depending upon the number of tourists on the dock. It was quite a change from loading general cargo and bulk oil to loading people. I began to think of the passengers as cargo. Each boat was equipped with a full service bar and a small snack bar. The crew consisted of one deckhand, who was usually a high school student. The lunch boat cruises were hectic and crowded with business types and tourists looking for temporary relief from the summer heat in the city. Saturday duty consisted of operating a similar vessel on a route through the waters of the outer harbor while giving a narrated tour of the islands. This tour included a brief history of each of the islands from colonial times to the present. After I was hired for the position I was given a small booklet to study, which described the most important historical events and interesting facts encountered along the route. It took some time to become accustomed to having passengers on board and making sure their needs were met.

Sunday was the busiest of the three days, because the trips were short and frequent. I usually completed eight trips in the inner harbor, each lasting forty-five minutes. This boat had only one propeller, which made it a challenge to maneuver around docked vessels as I made my way into the berthing slip. The large steering wheel was a traditional type made of varnished wood. I would be tired and hot after a summer day of literally going around in circles and dealing with the general public. Some days when I returned from the last scheduled trip of the day, I'd find a crowd of people standing on the dock and would know that at least one more trip was necessary, and perhaps more.

On one occasion while maneuvering out of the slip, I was turning the wheel quickly, which required considerable reaching and bending as I worked the wheel. As I released the wheel, it spun quickly, and one spoke caught me on the right cheek. I did not realize that my face was bleeding from the blow until my deckhand advised me that it might be a good idea to wash the blood off my cheek. I suppose that it would not reassure the passengers to see blood on the captain's face.

Occasionally it was necessary to make night cruises around the harbor in addition to the normal workday. Selling alcoholic beverages on board often created problems. One day as we were proceeding through the channel, we received a call from the captain of a passing vessel advising us that someone should go to the stern and check one of the passengers. The deckhand went to investigate and found an inebriated passenger sitting on the rail, in danger of falling overboard.

On the evening of the Fourth of July, I was assigned to transport a group of tourists to a nearby bay for the annual fireworks celebration. We left the dock early so that I could be sure of being able to position the boat to give those on board a good view. I chose not to anchor, which turned out to be a mistake, because I failed to anticipate having a hundred or so small boats anchor in close proximity. Walking to the stern at one point, I noticed a small motorboat with its anchor line leading under my vessel. The man on board was quite angry and yelled to me that his anchor line had become caught in our propeller. By that time I was so disgusted with the situation that I threw him a knife and told him to cut the line and call my boss in the morning.

It was a position that made me humble myself somewhat. Here I was with an unlimited Master's license, working with high school students. I even shared in the tips for the evening cruises. To add insult to injury, I was expected to assist with cleaning the boat after the passengers disembarked. Often this included washing vomit from the bulkheads and decks. It was usually so late by the time we had completed the cleaning process that I chose to remain on board, sleeping on a cot in the wheelhouse. It made no sense to drive forty-five minutes to home when I needed to be back on duty early in the morning. I remember arising from a very poor sleep and walking to the nearby waterfront area in search of a cup of coffee. I had to walk around the homeless in the streets as garbage trucks made their rounds picking up trash.

EXPEDITOR AND MARINE SURVEYOR

In my continuing quest to avoid returning to sea, I accepted a position as expeditor and loss-control specialist. I had never done this kind of thing, but I felt that my extensive experience on crude oil tankers had more than adequately prepared me for the job. A loss-control specialist and expeditor is one who is charged with the responsibility of supervising all aspects of bulk oil or bulk cargo loading and discharge. He or she is protecting the interests of the cargo or ship owner during all aspects of the cargo transfer. An expeditor does not make many friends, because he is attempting to ensure that the ship owner or terminal operator is following accepted practices and not trying to take short cuts with regard to operating procedures. This often involves sealing valves and flushing lines, which was not accepted practice at that time.

This position required me to travel extensively both within the United States and internationally, and it was frequently necessary to live on board vessels of all nationalities for several days at a time. While staying on board foreign vessels, I often had the opportunity to eat ethnic foods, but the food and sanitary conditions were poor on most assignments. The position required me to travel to a terminal and meet with the measurement representative and terminal representative. I supervised all measurements on the shore tanks. My primary responsibility was to ensure that the customer had received the same amount of oil at the final discharge port as had been loaded. When my submitted report showed a gain of oil,

235

the customer was pleased, but the opposite was true when a loss of oil was uncovered. In this case, it was always a challenge for me to explain the loss in transit. Many nights I would arrive at a terminal only to find that the ship's arrival had been delayed. The delay was rarely long enough to justify booking hotel accommodations, so I would nap in the car, waiting for the ship to arrive. I spent many cold winter nights that way, turning the car engine on and off to keep warm.

Once while observing a transfer of gasoline, I sensed a problem. The mate assured me that the operation was progressing normally, but a few minutes later I was convinced that things were not as they should be. A subsequent query produced the comment "fire!" Rushing to the lower level of the pumproom, I noticed a deckhand standing next to one of the main cargo pumps holding a garden hose. He was spraying a thin stream of water at a smoking pump casing, trying to prevent it from exploding. I rushed out of the pumproom and demanded the operation be shut down immediately. It was amazing that we did not have a major explosion that day.

On another occasion I flew to an oil platform several hundred miles offshore in the Gulf of Mexico, and lived with the workmen for five days. My duties included recording hourly readings on a computer screen that indicated the rate at which cargo was being transferred from a ship to the Louisiana Offshore Oil Platform. The LOOP, as it is more commonly known, is a major facility, having several submerged pipelines connected to mooring buoys. Ships moored to the buoys, attached to a floating hose, and began discharging cargo. Oil flowed from the vessel through the floating hose to the buoy, and thence to the sea floor, where it entered a pipeline leading to the platform. The final destination of the crude oil was a refinery, pipeline, or storage facility ashore. Another assignment took me to Montreal, Canada, to perform a vessel survey of an old bulk cement barge.

Each assignment required me to write a report during the operation. The final report was sent to the office and client each day. The first employer would only pay me when the company was paid for services rendered, but this unacceptable practice caused me major problems with cash flow. This was a key factor leading me to seek a similar position with another company based on Long Island, New York.

One assignment took me to a large refinery in Come by Chance, Newfoundland. It occurred to me that I would pass through a small fishing town, called Bay Bulls, where my old girlfriend, whom I met on the sea scout cruise, had lived as a child. I drove to a village store and inquired as to her whereabouts, learning that she no longer lived in Bay Bulls but that her sister lived just down the road. When she answered my knock on the door, she remembered exactly who I was. I learned that Marie had married and was living in California. I left a message for her to call me if she had a chance. A week later, as we were all sitting in the living room, the phone rang and Katelyn answered. She was surprised and said, "Mom, there is a woman on the phone for Dad and she has a foreign accent." It was good to talk to her and remember old times.

I used a computer to complete each client's final report then sent it through the telephone line to the company office. I didn't realize at the time that this was my introduction to the technology of e-mail and electronic message transfer. One embarrassing moment occurred as I was packing my equipment into the car. I leaned the company computer against one of the rear wheels of the car and returned to the house for more gear. I started the car and, as I backed up, sensed that I had driven over a rock. The rock turned out to be the computer. The most embarrassing aspect of that experience was the call to the company office, explaining the need for a new computer.

Sally and I tolerated this routine for four years as the stress built between us. It was not long before we decided that the job was not worth stressing our marriage to the breaking point. A year later it was again time for a change.

ANOTHER MOVE

Kirsten, our older daughter, was very much involved with the theater and loved acting when she attended high school. We learned that a nearby town had an excellent high school theater program. Life is a series of voyages, figuratively speaking, whether it is at sea or ashore, so it was off to a new family adventure. Katelyn entered the third grade and Kirsten enrolled in the high school. Both girls made many friends while we lived there, and we all enjoyed that brief period in our lives. During this time we hosted two Russian girls who were visiting the United States on a school tour from Russia.

Galia, our first visitor, did not speak English, and we did not speak Russian, which presented some interesting experiences and challenges. I was chosen to go to the high school to greet her and bring her to our home. I totally missed the fact that it was Halloween season. She entered our kitchen and saw a paper skeleton hanging over the kitchen table. The look of shock and loss of color on her face showed us all that Halloween must not be celebrated in Russia. I reassured her that Americans did not always hang skeletons over their dinner table. The following spring, our second Russian visitor, Helen, arrived. Communication was much easier with Helen, because she was fluent in English. On both occasions it was difficult to say goodbye when the time came for our visitor to board the bus for her return home. Our honeymoon to Russia many years before was beneficial to Sally and me, because we already had a visual image of the villages in their home country.

LIFE ON CAPE COD

After four years my family moved once again, this time to a small town on Cape Cod called Marstons Mills. Although I was still employed as a marine surveyor and loss-control specialist, it was obvious that another change in my employment was imminent. Being on call day and night had been taking a toll on my marriage, so I considered becoming a navigation instructor at a maritime academy in the area. Now I regretted having turned down the previous opportunity to teach at Maine Maritime Academy. After a short time, I became deck-training officer aboard the school's training ship on its annual training cruise. Over six weeks the vessel called at several ports in northern Europe. There was ample time in each port for us to go on tours and see the countryside. I had the opportunity to visit several cheese factories and enjoyed sitting beside the canals of Amsterdam.

A tragic event occurred as the training ship was departing port. During the undocking process, a cadet was injured while slacking a line to one of the assist tugs. I was not on watch at the time and am not privy to all the details of the incident, but the end result was the loss of one of his feet. This incident underscores the absolute need for all hands to be extremely vigilant while handling lines on deck.

During one summer, I taught seamanship and dock management to high school students from the inner city. It was a challenge to teach students who had never been in a boat how to row. The students were organized into three crews of eight, and

each student was presented with a large, heavy ash oar and told that he or she would become proficient at handling it by week's end. Propelling the heavy surfboat hull through the water required cooperation and teamwork. I welcomed the opportunity to expose these students to the ocean environment and to afford them the chance to realize what they could achieve if they worked together as a team. Most of the students did not believe that they would actually be able to move a boat that heavy with just oars and their combined strength. When all of them rowed in unison, they expressed their amazement at how fast the boat traveled through the water. Another aspect of this program was to introduce the students to splicing rope, tying knots, and performing basic coastal navigation in the classroom ashore.

Living on Cape Cod was a new experience for several reasons. The environment was very different from Cape Ann, which had been my lifelong home. Travel to and from Boston involved crossing one of two highway bridges that were clogged with traffic much of the time. The seamanship program ended after several weeks, and it was time for me to find some other part-time employment as I continued to sort out my life.

An opportunity arose at a small private school. I was to teach mapping, which was similar to land surveying, using triangulation methods. During the initial interview, the administrators mentioned that the students would need a few days to unpack. I envisioned each student arriving from a different location in the country and unpacking his or her bags, an activity that would take an hour or so, but they were actually referring to the process of going into the attic of a large building and bringing many boxes downstairs. I understood that the boxes contained the materials for the summer program, and at the end of August the process was reversed, when the boxes were repacked and returned to the attic for another winter. I could see that the quandary of what I could do ashore for employment was rearing its ugly head once again. I worked on my resumé, attempting to tweak it so that I would be able to sell myself for a shoreside position. The job search process was always painful for me, so I constantly searched for a way to avoid it. Sally suggested that I give some thought to teaching science, because I would make a "dynamite science teacher." There was an opening for a teaching assistant position at a vocational technical high school in the area, and even though it was not a science position, I looked at it as a way of getting my feet wet in the world of education.

Even though I did not possess a formal teaching certification at the time, I was hired, having no idea of what lay ahead. The routine consisted of reporting to a supervisor at the beginning of the day for my day's assignment, which might be in the classroom or in one of the many technical shops. On one assignment I was placed in the auto body shop and instructed to prevent two students from coming into physical contact with one another during the day. On another assignment I observed students during a class in United States history. The teacher was reading to the students, which surprised me. When I asked him why he was reading from the text, he asked if I was going to be in his next class. Halfway through that class, he asked one of the students to read a passage from the text aloud, and it quickly became apparent what he meant by his comment. This particular student read the passage with a great deal of difficulty. I never knew from one day to the next what was in store for me.

Sally soon directed my attention to the fact that a local middle school was in need of a long-term substitute teacher of science. When I asked her about the qualifications required, she explained that a formal teaching certificate was not required for a substitute position. With that in mind, I applied and was asked to come in for an interview, during which the principal asked how I felt about dissecting frogs. I replied that I had never dissected one, but if it was part of the curriculum, then bring on the frogs.

Apparently the principal liked my answer, because I was hired for the position, and the following week I began my introduction to formal public education. I was off and running on a new career, the duration of which remained a mystery. My duties consisted of teaching a general course in science to eighth-grade students for the remainder of the school year. I had only a week to brush up on atoms, the periodic table, food chains, physics, environmental science, and much more.

On the first morning of my new employment, I contemplated the impact of what I had just done. As I stood at the front of the classroom and gazed over the rows of empty desks, I tried to imagine what it would be like to be in control of three classes, each consisting of twenty-five eighth-graders. How was I going to remember seventy-five names in the first week? Who would assist me with learning the skills of classroom management? I did not know where to begin. It took hours of preparation during the first several weeks to review the curriculum material that I would be teaching. Much of the time I struggled to stay 24 hours ahead of the students in content knowledge. As I reviewed and organized the material, however, I could see that the practical experience I had gained during my years at sea would be extremely beneficial to me.

Sally helped me understand the methods and skills required

to teach students with varied learning styles. A large part of teaching today is spent in the preparation of lesson plans that will satisfy the needs of students with special educational needs. Many schools supply a teaching assistant to assist the classroom teacher with the implementation of these specialized lesson plans, but I was alone in the classroom and often felt overwhelmed by my many and varied duties. Much of my available planning time was taken up with organizing the classroom into learning centers and installing rules and procedures for maintaining discipline. It was a pleasure to interact with most of the students, but there were some unpleasant moments.

The inevitable week arrived midway during the school year when I was to begin the unit on frog dissection. On Friday afternoon I went to the biology teacher's classroom, knocked gently on her door, and said that I was "in trouble." When she inquired as to the reason for my concern, I explained that I was to begin teaching my students about frog dissection during the next week. She suggested that I get a dead frog, which had been preserved, from the science lab and bring it back to her classroom. A short time later, I walked into her room with frog in hand, ready to begin my crash course. "Now," she said, "we will begin and you are going to do it." She explained the process of removing the eyeballs, which I found disgusting. Each day I was to return for training in removal of the skin from the legs and then the serious work of sorting through the internal organs. After beginning this crash course, I prepared the necessary materials on Saturday and Sunday for my new, challenging assignment.

On Monday morning I conducted my class as though I was fully familiar with the frog dissection process. As soon as the bell rang at the end of each day, I would return to the biology teacher for the next installment of my preparation for the following day's lesson. I was very relieved when the last lesson was completed on Friday. The dissection unit required each student to paste the organs of their frog into a folder made of construction paper, a step I found to be disgusting and unnecessary. Once a student asked about the procedure for disposal of waste parts, and I told him to throw them into the wastebasket and the janitor would take care of it. I was not aware at the time that the frog parts were considered biologically harmful. The temporary substitute position lasted approximately eight months, until the end of the school year. I could not apply for a full-time position for the following year because I did not hold a formal teaching certificate.

Deciding to look into the requirements for becoming a fully certified science teacher, I learned that I would have to complete several courses in education in order to earn a provisional certificate and would then have to acquire a Master's Degree in Education within five years. The following winter I attended education courses at a nearby college. After a winter of course work and a summer spent working several jobs, I applied for and received a teaching certification, and was awarded a position at the same middle school where I had worked previously. I was excited to be returning to the same classroom and began to prepare for what turned out to be a rewarding and enjoyable school year. The following year, however, I was notified that I would not be rehired due to the fact that layoffs were necessary and I did not have tenure or "permanent status." The issue of tenure is a problem today in many school systems. Teachers who do not have the required number of years experience (usually three) are the first to have their employment terminated, regardless of qualifications or performance.

Often we find ourselves in a position where it is necessary to accept employment below our qualifications in order to provide an income. I was now in such a position and knew that I would have to find temporary local work. I worked as a floor person at a local hardware store, answering customer's questions and assisting where needed. For a short period of time I worked as a rigger at a local yacht yard. I tried to learn all I could from each of these experiences.

As soon as we moved to Cape Cod, I had joined a local yacht club that emphasized sailing, and now I asked several of the members if they had any knowledge of employment opportunities. A notice on the club bulletin board stated that a crewmember was needed for a racing sailboat for the weekend races. I answered the notice and got a berth for the summer. A person was needed to paint the trim on the yacht club building, so I contracted with the club and began working on a part-time basis. While painting the club building, I met a man who ran a small boatyard and decided to work with him whenever the opportunity presented itself. The work consisted of painting, moving, and launching small boats, setting moorings, and occasionally painting the yard owner's house. The person with whom I sailed on weekends lived in a large old wooden home overlooking the harbor, and he occasionally needed a general handyman on his property. This was a mutually beneficial situation, resulting in still another part-time job.

My work estimate for painting the yacht club was much lower than it should have been. I badly underestimated the number of man-hours necessary to complete the work, which reduced the compensation that should have been paid. When my weekend skipper left for his winter home out of state, he left a work list for me to attend to. This worked out well toward the end of our time on the cape. I was working an alternate three-week schedule on board a tugboat in Puerto Rico, and I was able to perform the handyman work during the weeks when I was at home.

It was great to crew in the weekend races over the course of several summers. The most exciting race took place at a regatta held at Edgartown, on the island of Martha's Vineyard. The day before the regatta, we sailed the boat to Edgartown from the mainland of Cape Cod. On regatta day we all piled into a small outboard motorboat with the intention of going to the race site, having lunch, and then racing in the afternoon. The sea was extremely rough as we set out from Oyster Harbor, causing considerable concern on my part regarding what might lie ahead for the day's sailing. As we ate our lunches on the boat at the mooring, we discussed the weather conditions. The skipper asked me what I thought about racing under the existing conditions. I replied, "I think you are all crazy if you race today, but I'm signed on as crew and if we decide to race, I'm in." He disregarded my comments, and we prepared to get underway for the starting line. The wind had risen to a velocity of twenty-five to thirty knots by the time we sailed down the channel.

The starting line was set so that the boats would sail downwind toward the first mark. This method of starting races is not usually followed because of the danger of the boats being too close together as they cross the starting line, often with spinnakers flying. The strong wind and rough sea made the situation even more dangerous. After tense pre-start maneuvers, the gun sounded and the boats squared off with spinnakers set, heading toward the first mark. Only minutes after crossing the line, our spinnaker pole broke in the middle under the heavy compression loads, but we managed to keep the spinnaker full and drawing without the pole. As the boat approached the end of the first downwind leg, the mark was nowhere in sight. It was clear to all of us that the leeward mark had dragged anchor and washed up on the beach. The race committee, realizing that there was no leeward mark, declared the race over. I knew right then that the day was destined to be one in which we all would have been better advised to remain on the mooring.

I had noticed a small inflatable boat with several people on board, following our course during the first leg. One person appeared to be hastily snapping pictures of our frenetic efforts to remain in one piece while searching for the missing mark. I did not give it a second thought, as my preeminent thoughts were of survival without any of us sustaining injuries or falling over the side. Later, in October, as I was picking up the mail, I noticed that the latest issue of *Sail* magazine had arrived, and my attention was immediately drawn to a picture of a small sailboat sailing downwind in a wild sea. The bow wave was white with froth, which is the condition referred to when someone says that a boat "has a bone in her teeth." The boat appeared to be jumping from one wave to the next as the crew struggled to keep it under control. Recognizing the number on the spinnaker, I realized that it was our boat on the cover. The skipper made up a computer copy of the picture with bubble captions coming out of each of our mouths, faithfully capturing things we had said during that day. All of us received one of these pictures as a Christmas present.

When it was apparent that the race had been called off for the day, we took in the spinnaker, hardened up close on the wind, and headed back toward the channel. My duties included handling the mainsheet, which is the line that controls the large mainsail. It was hard work under heavy wind conditions such as these, and it often took time to get all of the line in. We were extremely tired and tense as the boat slammed into each wave, propelled by headwinds of about thirty knots. We finally arrived at the mooring location and calmer seas, but the wind was still blowing hard. As we rounded up into the wind and approached the mooring buoy, the running backstay wire became snagged on the centerboard cleat. All efforts to free the wire were in vain as the pressure on the boom increased. The pressure was concentrated in one place on the boom, resulting in a sharp bang as the boom fractured. After securing the boat and gear at the mooring, the skipper looked at me and said, "I think you were right about not going out today."

THE GULL TAKES TO THE AIR

During my earlier days at the yacht club in Rockport, I had acquired the nickname of "Gull"—the reason why I am not certain. Some of my friends still refer to me as Gull. Our home in Marstons Mills was located next to a small, grass-covered airfield that contained many rough spots. Driving home one day, I passed the airfield and noticed a glider and its tow plane standing near the road. I pulled my truck over and asked if they accepted a credit card. When the pilot answered in the affirmative, I told him that I was ready to sign on. There were no lessons involved in this experience. I just climbed into the glider, hooked up the safety straps, and was ready to go. The pilot sat behind me in the narrow cockpit.

After a few minutes, the tow wire was connected and we were ready to be towed aloft for some soaring. In order to keep the glider's wing tip from touching the ground during takeoff, the pilot's wife ran alongside us holding the wing as we gathered speed down the runway. Eventually, both aircraft cleared the ground and began a slow climb to about four thousand feet. When the time was right, the pilot instructed me to push my left foot down on a yellow lever, which was located on the cockpit floor. He yelled back to me that I was free to open the window and put my arm out. We were only going about thirty-five miles per hour and could hear the voices on the ground. Now I knew what that quiet object was high in the air over our home that had been reflecting sunlight in my direction.

The flight lasted approximately thirty minutes and was incredible fun. As we prepared to descend to the airport for our landing, it was necessary to lose a substantial amount of altitude rather quickly. In order to do that, the pilot began to send the aircraft into a series of spirals. I quickly informed him that I would become extremely sick if this condition continued, so the flight plan was changed "on the fly." This was a fantastic experience that I will not soon forget.

A few years later, Sally and I were in La Jolla, California, and noticed a sign that read, "Torrey Pines Glider Port." The "Gull" felt the urge to become airborne once again, and I suggested that we drive to the field and watch the action just for the fun of it. As I watched people sitting comfortably in their harnesses under gaily-colored parachutes, the urge to give it a try grew stronger. By the time I had worked myself up to doing it, however the wind had decreased to the point where the person in charge deemed the conditions marginal for a person of my weight. I had no problem waiting until the next day, because I felt that running off a 350-foot-high cliff was not something to try under questionable conditions.

The next morning I awoke in our nearby hotel room to find a steady sea breeze coming toward the cliffs. I informed Sally that this was the day and called the airfield office. They gave me the green light and off we went. I fully expected to be required to take a few lessons prior to running off the edge of a cliff with a total stranger, but when I asked my pilot about lessons, he told me that he was headed to the van to get a harness and that no lessons were necessary. After being securely buckled into the harness, I was told to hold the parachute while it filled with air. Once it had filled, we both pulled hard and ran as fast as we could. At the instant that I cleared the cliff, I felt his knee pushing me into the harness seat, and the chute began to lift on the updraft. It was a truly wonderful experience, one that I did not want to end. As we soared up and down the cliff rim, we noticed a hawk gliding on a parallel course. The pilot mentioned that the same hawk joined him each day in about the same spot.

These experiences were so great that I have given some thought to jumping out of a plane and attempting to sky dive. My daughter Katelyn has done it in Australia and said that it is fantastic. I have not built up to the point of making a call, but it is not far away. I think the paragliding experience was easier because the parachute was full prior to jumping from the cliff. In sky diving, there is an element of doubt as to whether the parachute will open. I am still working on that one.

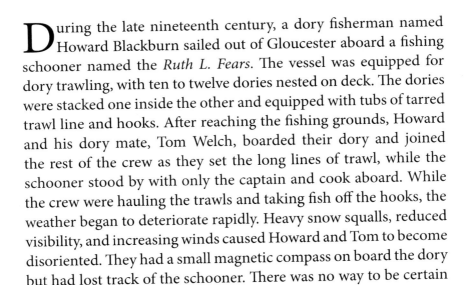

THE BLACKBURN CHALLENGE

During the late nineteenth century, a dory fisherman named Howard Blackburn sailed out of Gloucester aboard a fishing schooner named the *Ruth L. Fears*. The vessel was equipped for dory trawling, with ten to twelve dories nested on deck. The dories were stacked one inside the other and equipped with tubs of tarred trawl line and hooks. After reaching the fishing grounds, Howard and his dory mate, Tom Welch, boarded their dory and joined the rest of the crew as they set the long lines of trawl, while the schooner stood by with only the captain and cook aboard. While the crew were hauling the trawls and taking fish off the hooks, the weather began to deteriorate rapidly. Heavy snow squalls, reduced visibility, and increasing winds caused Howard and Tom to become disoriented. They had a small magnetic compass on board the dory but had lost track of the schooner. There was no way to be certain of which direction to row in order to reach the *Fears*.

When it became apparent that they were lost, Howard knew that their only chance for survival was to row toward shore, which would take several days under ideal conditions. After a short time, Mr. Welch succumbed to the wet and cold and froze to death. Howard pushed on toward the coast of Nova Scotia, periodically taking breaks to bail. While bailing the seawater from the dory, he lost his gloves over the side. He immersed his hands in the cold seawater and curled his fingers around the oar handles, allowing them to freeze in a rowing position. This would enable him to

continue rowing and bail when necessary. After several days, he sighted shore and noticed a fisherman's cabin in the distance. After landing the dory and trudging through waist-high snow and biting cold, he reached the cabin. The fisherman and his wife nursed Howard back to good health, but not before he lost most of his fingers and toes and part of one thumb.

In honor of Howard's enduring spirit and determination to survive, a long-distance rowing race called the Blackburn Challenge was initiated. This twenty-mile long race circumnavigates Cape Ann and is open to all rowing craft. I have enjoyed rowing for most of my life and became interested in this challenge. I had purchased a twelve-foot-long rowboat for our daughter Kirsten when she was three years old, and we used it in Rockport Harbor when she was a little girl. It had been out of the water for many years when I decided to participate in the Blackburn Challenge. Kirsten was in high school, and the boat was stored inside an old barn in our backyard. On the night before the Blackburn Challenge, some of Kirsten's friends were having pizza at our house. During the evening, I mentioned to some of the boys that I wanted to participate in the Blackburn Challenge but could not get the boat into the water in time for it to swell. They offered to help me load it into the truck so that I could take it to Gloucester, launch it, and race on the following day.

Caught up in the moment, I went along with the plan, thinking that the leaking would not be a serious problem. The next morning I arrived at the launch ramp and put the boat in the water. It leaked badly, of course, because it had been out of the water for so long, but I didn't let that bother me because I was caught up with the excitement of the race, the people, and the many different kinds of rowing boats.

It was a calm morning as we lined up at the starting line. The various classes of boats started at five-minute intervals. The first three miles took us down the Annisquam River and into Ipswich Bay. I had to stop and bail the boat every ten or fifteen minutes in order to stay afloat. The Gap between Sraitsmouth Island and the mainland off Rockport is the halfway point of the course, and it was there that participants had to decide whether to continue on to the finish line in Gloucester Harbor or leave the competition.

Satisfied that I had successfully rowed a distance of approximately ten miles under frustrating conditions, I notified the chase boat that I intended to quit the race and proceed into Rockport Harbor to haul the boat at the yacht club. I was at a distinct disadvantage because of the length of my boat and its excessive leaking. The longer its waterline length, the faster a boat will go through the water. Looking back, it amazes me that I thought I could row twenty miles after doing nothing to condition my body beforehand. This race showed me that under the right circumstances, I could go all the way. The year was 1991, and I knew that I was hooked and would return for another attempt.

I have participated in the Blackburn Challenge nine times now, managing to finish the course three times, twice in a fixed-seat craft and once in a sliding-seat peapod. My finishing time with the fixed-seat rowboats was approximately 5 hours, 35 minutes, and I finished in 4 hours, 24 minutes in the peapod. In each of the other six races, I reached the halfway point for a distance of ten miles. It is at that point that the wind typically picks up from the southwest, the seas begin to build, and I feel completely played out.

The course from Thacher Island to Eastern Point is long and grueling, with no harbors in which to seek refuge. The rower becomes very tired and frustrated as the wind increases from the southwest and the seas build from dead ahead. As the boats pass Eastern Point and round the end of Dog Bar Breakwater, they must contend with large wakes from whale-watching boats and commercial fishing boats. During one race, I was rowing a fixed-seat skiff at a point about five hundred yards from the finish line when a member of the race committee hailed me with a loud speaker to ask if I was all right. I knew immediately that I must sharpen up my stroke and look alive, because I must have appeared very ragged. I was really hurting at the time, but I knew that I would be able to complete the race. Following the finish, I managed to row to a nearby beach and pull the boat out of the water. I was barely able to climb from the boat without assistance. As I lay on my back in the hot sun, totally exhausted, a man approached and offered me an ice-cold beer, which I could not refuse.

While we lived on Cape Cod, I became interested in ocean sculls. I learned about rowing sliding-seat craft by watching my younger daughter, Katelyn, practice with the high school rowing team. I purchased a second-hand scull and began rowing on small lakes and ponds, where the water was calm most of the time. It was easy to transport the scull atop the custom roof rack on my truck. I could carry it over my head to the launch site and not have to rely on help from others when launching and hauling.

Later, when my family returned to live on Cape Ann, I decided that the scull was not seaworthy enough for the ocean. Once I attempted to row it in the Blackburn Challenge but became apprehensive as I rounded Halibut Point. The sea and swells were steadily building, and I was slowly being swept closer to the rocky shoreline. On another occasion I miscalculated the time of slack water and found myself under a local drawbridge, struggling against a strong head current and tide rip. There was a lobster boat following me immediately astern through the bridge opening, and I was apprehensive that I would lose control and be swept back into the lobster boat's propeller, possibly suffering serious injury. Because of the insecure feeling of using the scull on the ocean, I was driving thirty minutes each day to find calm water on the only lake nearby. This was unacceptable, and it was time to locate a more seaworthy boat.

Accordingly I purchased a 16-foot fiberglass boat designed along the lines of a traditional Maine peapod. I traded my scull for the peapod but kept the sliding seat rowing unit. Now I was ready to attempt rowing the Blackburn Challenge with a more competitive and safer boat. During the winter of 2009/2010, I worked out with the assistance of a friend as personal trainer. My goal was to adequately condition my body so that I would be able to endure the punishment and complete the course with a respectable time. I kept the boat at a marina along the shore of the Annisquam River, which gave me the opportunity to train on calm waters.

As I trained on the treadmill, I developed a slight back pain, which later increased in intensity during heavier workouts on the river. The pain eased when I rowed, but it became more severe when I was not rowing. Race day arrived, and the weather conditions were absolutely perfect. I knew that all conditions pointed to a respectable finishing time for the day. During the race, I took breaks at regular intervals to prevent dehydration and took in small amounts of food. My finishing time of 4 hours, 24 minutes was very respectable. Although I finished last in my class, I was happy and proud to have completed the course.

I may not be able to attempt this grueling test again, because I was recently diagnosed with spinal stenosis. I may downgrade my goal in the spring to one six-mile race in the Essex River. This is the first time that I have been subjected to chronic pain, and it has made me realize that I may not be able to do the things I did many years ago. I went to a local hospital for a radio frequency treatment, which was successful. There has been no appreciable pain in the past several months. I will begin working out on the rowing machine in the spring, in order to stay in good physical condition and control my weight. If my work schedule allows and I am not feeling debilitating pain, I may attempt the Blackburn Challenge one more time.

ANOTHER COURSE CHANGE

When I was a young boy, I listened to a story about a father, a son, and a toy tugboat on my parents' record player until the record became so scratched that it could barely be understood. My favorite book was a classic children's book called *Scuffy the Tug Boat*. During that time period, a fishing dragger ran aground and sank offshore. The salvage operation involved a large wooden barge equipped with a derrick and tended by an old wooden tugboat. The salvage crew towed the derelict hull to Front Beach, grounding it on the sand at high water. Repairs were performed on the hull during periods of low water. I enjoyed going to the beach behind my house and watching the tug maneuver as it positioned the barge. On still another occasion, I watched, with intense interest as an old wooden tug assisted a dredging operation in the inner harbor of Rockport. This was the beginning of my lifetime fascination for tugboats.

Many years have passed since that time, but my interest in the towing industry is as strong as ever. In September 1997, I informed Sally that I wanted to acquire knowledge and experience about tugs and the towing industry. This was the only branch of the maritime industry that I had not tried, having served on break-bulk freighters, tankers, coastal vessels, and sail-training vessels. Understanding that my interest in tugs dated back to my childhood years, Sally urged me to "follow your dream." She has always supported me in whatever I have done, even though some of these endeavors have been less successful than others.

I learned of a company that operated two tugs on the south coast of Puerto Rico and was in need of an AB/tankerman. The AB/tankerman is in charge of the cargo operations on board the barge. While the barge is being towed, he or she performs the functions of a deckhand, which include painting, chipping rust, replacing tire fenders, general cleaning, and other necessary duties. The key aspects of the deckhand's duties are handling the shock line and making the tug fast alongside the barge and dock. It was essential to learn these procedures, because once I became qualified, my primary responsibility would be the safety of the crew. Regardless of my extensive shipboard experience as a deck officer, it was necessary to begin on deck, gradually working my way into the wheelhouse.

It was going to be difficult to swallow my pride, considering that I was licensed as Master of Steam and Motor Vessels of Unlimited Tonnage Upon Oceans. Beginning at the bottom was essential, however, due to the unique nature of the job description. There was a definite possibility of injuring myself, or a fellow crewmember if I did not undergo the necessary training. The work on deck was physical at times, handling mooring lines and climbing to and from the barge. I wondered whether my aging body would measure up to the challenge. I looked forward to the experience with excitement and some trepidation, not knowing what challenges lay ahead. I reported on board a tug in Yabucoa, a port on the south coast of Puerto Rico. I was accustomed to hard work, so I dove right in with the intention of learning the ropes quickly, thereby minimizing the time necessary to advance to the wheelhouse. The cargo-related duties came easily once I learned the layout of the barge, given that I had supervised the loading and discharging of large tankers.

I was surprised to see that the daily routines on board tugboats and ships contrast sharply. On a tug, the watch officer is permitted to sit in a chair and play music while on duty. Both of these practices are not allowed on board ships, probably because it could contribute to the watch stander being less alert than is required. The previous comment notwithstanding, it did not take me long to become accustomed to these new freedoms. All hands work together as a team when there is a large job to perform, such as loading groceries or stores or performing engine repairs. There is a definite class hierarchy on board ships, and I recall my instructors warning me that "familiarity breeds contempt" and emphasizing that the officers and crew of a ship should not become too friendly. I feel that each officer ought to be able to use sound judgment when determining the advisability of this practice. In any event, this hierarchy is much less pronounced on tugs.

The tug and its assigned barge ran between the ports of Guayanilla, Aguirre, and Yabucoa, Puerto Rico. Most of the loading was done in Guayanilla, and usually the cargo was delivered to Aguirre, with an occasional delivery to Yabucoa or San Juan. When there were no orders for the tug and barge, crewmembers performed maintenance at their respective lay berths. This was convenient, because it allowed crewmembers to leave the boat for walks along the shore or into town.

Walking along the paths toward a nearby beach, I often passed cows grazing in the fields. Once I passed a large, ominous-looking bull standing amid a herd of docile cows. His behavior and manner made it clear to me that I was not wanted, convincing me to pick up my pace immediately. The privacy of the beach was especially nice because it allowed me to lie in the sun and relax. It is always better to get away from the boat once in a while and collect one's thoughts. Tensions occasionally develop among the crew due to the confined conditions and the long period of time on duty. I had little in common with most of the crewmembers, with one exception—the engineer. He and I got along well because of our many common interests. We enjoyed going on walks and discussing current events. We still maintain that friendship today through periodic telephone conversations, an occasional beer, or a trip to a nearby bookstore. This was a welcome change for me, as I did not seem to share the interests of many of my fellow crewmembers.

The use of a shock line when towing a barge astern was one aspect of the operation that was totally unfamiliar to me. A heavy tow wire is attached to a towing winch on the tug, where the wire is stored on a large drum. The winch controls used to lengthen and shorten the towing wire are located on the deck above the main deck. A chain bridle forming a Y configuration leads from the port and starboard bows of the barge to a short length of chain. When towing astern, the tow wire is shackled to a heavy line eighty to one hundred feet in length. This line connects the tow wire and the chain "pigtail" coming from the Y of the bridle. When shortening tow, the tow wire can only be heaved in as far as the towing shackle connected to the line. The line is then taken in with the aid of a winch drum and much hard work. This was a demanding physical job in the heat, requiring a deckhand to lean over the stern of the tug and attach a rope "choker" around the shock line. A messenger line was then connected to the "choker" and used to take in the shock line in bights. This process was repeated several times until the barge was near enough to the tug to allow close maneuverability.

During my first year working as AB/tankerman, I was anxious to handle the tug underway but had not been given that opportunity. At the end of that year, a new captain was assigned to the tug. One day as I was on the bow preparing to let go the lines, I waited for word to cast off. I called up to the wheelhouse and asked when we were letting go, the captain replied, "When you come up here and drive." I wasted no time climbing the ladder to the wheelhouse, because I knew that I could handle the boat if given the opportunity. I maneuvered the tug away from the dock and alongside the barge without incident. The captain must have been impressed, because a week later he gave me the opportunity to make the tug up alongside the barge, and shortly after that I got to undock the loaded barge and transit the channel.

The duties of a tankerman are the same as the duties of a tanker mate except that the pipelines, pumps, and related equipment are on a much smaller scale. The job was more physically challenging than being a chief officer because it involved climbing up the side of a light barge by means of "pigeon holes" and handling mooring lines. As with any new position, there were additional factors to be aware of. One afternoon while we were loading the barge, the captain informed me that the loaded amount would be cut short and that we would need to sail the barge as soon as possible. As the independent inspector and I were completing the paperwork, I closed the large, heavy window in the front part of the barge deckhouse from the inside. Attempting to save time, I reached up and removed the metal strut that supported the window without realizing that my left thumb was draped over the sharp metal sill at the bottom of the window frame. I lost my hold on the window, causing it to fall and trap my thumb. I returned to the tug and showed my friend what had happened, at which time he replied, "What did you do that for? That will get you a couple of weeks off." I knew he was right. It was two weeks before it had healed well enough for me to return to the tug.

After working on deck for two years, I began a mate-training program sponsored by the company. The first step in the process was for the trainees to gain experience on a bridge simulator. Upon completion of the simulator training, it was time for "hands on" training aboard several company tugs. The first day consisted of handling a small tug in several real-life situations while taking current and wind into consideration.

On one occasion as I was approaching the dock in push gear, the deckhand on the bow of the barge warned me that I was going too fast and was heading directly toward the dock. I tried to twist the barge away from the dock instead of taking way off. I should have stopped, regrouped, and tried a different approach strategy. I was surprised that the captain watched me the entire time and didn't give suggestions to prevent an incident. Perhaps he was nervous that if he took over and we made contact with the dock, he would be held responsible. The barge made contact with the dock and I was removed from the program. I was then reassigned as tankerman on board a manned barge, a blow to my pride as well as my self-confidence. The living conditions on this barge were marginal to say the least. One cold midnight in Carteret, New Jersey, with the thermometer reading zero degrees, I was instructed to go ashore for groceries. After hefting the groceries from the carts to the cab and then from the cab to the dock, it was necessary to carry them over a pipeline and down the length of a 300-foot wooden pier. The last step was to transfer them from the dock to the barge. After everything was loaded aboard, the barge captain criticized me for breaking one egg and crushing a loaf of bread. This was the final straw. I knew it was time to make another change.

A NEW TUGBOAT COMPANY

While I was in Philadelphia, the two tugs in Puerto Rico were sold to another company. Prior to my participation in the mate-training program, the representative in charge of Puerto Rican operations for the purchasing company had advised me to sign on with them as mate, and those words were fresh in my memory as I carried those groceries down the pier. The new fleet consisted of four tugs, the two additional boats having been operating in the Gulf of Mexico for several years. I was hired immediately as mate and reported for duty.

After working as mate for several years, the resignation of one of the captains presented an opportunity for me. My vessel had been running from Guayanilla to Aguirre for the most part, and due to the regularity of this run, I had gained the necessary number of piloting trips in and out of both ports. This made it possible for me to fit into the captain position. The manager of operations had observed me docking the loaded barge on several occasions, often commenting on my skill at handling the boat and barge. As we were preparing to sail from Aguirre one afternoon, he asked me if I was interested in sailing as captain.

I was excited but a bit apprehensive when I considered the increased responsibility the position entailed. As the crew prepared to undock the light barge, I stood in the upper wheelhouse, thinking about the fact that I was realizing a dream of many years. Leaving the dock in Aguirre is challenging due to the prevailing onshore wind in the afternoon. The tug is backed on a springline to get the bow swinging away from the dock. As soon as the wind is slightly on the port bow of the barge, left rudder is applied and the throttles are shifted ahead. At this time the springline is let go, the rudder put amidships, and the barge is driven ahead until clear of the dock. Once clear of the dock, right rudder is applied and the barge is driven into the middle of the harbor. When clear of the anchorage, the maneuver to string out the barge on the tow wire astern is performed, and the vessel is navigated down the channel. All these maneuvers I performed successfully.

Upon the approach to a port, usually in the vicinity of the sea buoy, the tow wire is shortened to a more manageable length. When the tug is ready to make up alongside the barge, headway is reduced and the barge is headed into the wind. It is then necessary to turn the tug 180 degrees to go alongside the barge. Headlines and springs are made up, and the tow wire is tightened aft. This is the method used to maneuver the barge in close-quarters situations. Particular caution must be exercised while doing this maneuver to ensure that the tow wire does not pass under the tug from the outboard side. There is always the possibility of someone being injured on deck. All such factors must be the primary concern of the person in charge, and I juggled them all successfully on the approach to Guayanilla that day. Aguirre is a small village tucked among mangrove swamps on the central southern coast of Puerto Rico. The first time I had approached the dock, I had noticed what seemed to be a very laid-back atmosphere among the dock personnel. As the barge neared the dock, I spotted two men in a small skiff with an outboard motor on the stern, slowly making their way toward us. They came from a small wooden dock that jutted out from the shoreline of the sleepy village, and it turned out that they were the people responsible to make the barge fast, place and secure the oil boom around the barge, and connect the cargo hose. These two men were a sharp contrast to what I had been accustomed to seeing. They were usually unshaven and wore shower togs instead of safety shoes. This was my introduction to

Jimmy and Rey, the "Aguirre Boom Guys." Each time we arrived in Aguirre, they were friendly and accommodating. Often they invited us to accompany them in their small boat to the mangrove swamps for snorkeling trips or to the village to obtain groceries and supplies.

The people in Aguirre appeared to live a very relaxed and stress-free life. I took leisurely walks through town in the evenings when I could get off the tug. There were chickens in many yards and lots of dogs. Many years before, there had been a sugar plant in the village, now defunct, and housing had been provided to the workers of the plant. When the plant ceased to operate, the homes were left to the workers. The only source of employment today in Aguirre is a large power plant. Those in the village who do not work at the plant pass their time from day to day with leisure hours fishing or sitting in the shade of nearby trees shooting the breeze, picking up work whenever the opportunity presents itself.

Eventually, my tug and its barge were dispatched to New York Harbor. Once we arrived, I thought that the tug would stand by the barge as in Guayanilla, but I was wrong. After securing the barge at the company dock, the tug came under the supervision of the dispatcher. He had us running without letup after that, moving barges, performing ship assists, and doing whatever else was required. New York Harbor is a chaotic place at times. Three VHF radios must be monitored at all times when working in the port. This was extremely difficult for me due to an apparent auditory processing problem. Multiple audio inputs distract me to the point that it all sounds like noise. Once the captain became frustrated because of this issue and said, "They are calling you. Don't you hear them?" Well, I heard lots of noise and could not differentiate our call above all the other stimuli on the radio.

ANOTHER MOVE FOR THE FAMILY

At about this time, Katelyn, our younger daughter, had finished high school on Cape Cod. We all realized how much we missed Cape Ann, so the decision was made to move back to Rockport. I went to Cape Ann while Sally was on a business trip to locate temporary housing while we searched for a more permanent house. After meeting an old friend, I found a unique apartment on Bearskin Neck. This is the area of town where the tourist shops and art galleries are centrally located. The outstanding feature of the apartment was the view of the ocean and harbor from the second and third floors. Each evening we sat by the picture window and relaxed while watching the sunset. There were features of this apartment that were frustrating, such as the drafty windows and the outside stairway. Gretel, our golden retriever, was getting along in years by this time and having difficulty walking. It was painful to watch her slowly climb the stairway. She was diagnosed with bone cancer and euthanized shortly after we moved in. We loved Gretel with all our hearts, and it killed us to part with her.

Sally and I will always remember the cold wind seeping through the openings around the windows. It seemed like a never-ending task to stop the drafts from entering the room. I particularly remember the days carrying groceries up that outside stairway in a cold northwest wind. The inside required some painting and sprucing up. Often I was in Rockport painting while Sally was living in our home in Marstons Mills.

On the morning of September 11, 2001, Sally called to tell me about a building having been hit by a jet plane in New York. I turned on the television just as a second plane was crashing into one of the World Trade Center towers. Later broadcasts reported the hijacking of two additional planes, one of which hit the Pentagon while the other crashed in a remote field in Pennsylvania. It was clear to us both that this was a terrorist attack and that our world would never be the same.

We eventually found a house with a large yard on Main Street, the road that leads into town. We planted Arbor vitae bushes along the wall in front and purchased a shed for our lawn equipment. The house was too small for all of our things and Sally's educational consulting business, but we struggled on for several years, trying to make it work. Finally the cars and trucks passing by on their way into town created so much road noise that the situation became unacceptable. We put the house on the market and were fortunate to sell it after waiting two years.

After an extensive search, we located a house on a dirt road with lots of woods and a large yard near the center of town. No major work was needed because it had recently been renovated. During the time that we lived in these two homes, my career path was pointing me in the direction of teaching science once again.

THACHER ISLAND ASSOCIATION

I decided that I would do some community service when the family was settled in our new house. I had previously served on the Rockport School Committee for one year and had become involved in several controversial issues during that time. This time I was determined to volunteer for a fairly benign but enjoyable local cause. Because my heritage was so deep rooted in the sea and maritime affairs, it made sense that I should find a maritime-related organization.

The Thacher Island Association was just the thing for me. Thacher Island is about one-half mile offshore to the east of the town of Rockport. It can be easily reached from Rockport Harbor by boat or directly from the nearby shoreline by boat or kayak. There are two lighthouses on the island positioned in a north-to-south orientation. Both towers are equipped with lights, which are operational today. The south tower light is maintained by the United States Coast Guard and is a listed navigational aid. The light in the north tower is maintained by the Thacher Island Association and is powered by a solar-powered light that is visible for a distance of six miles.

The original lighthouses were constructed in their present locations in 1771 and were 45 feet high. The present towers were constructed in 1861 and are 124 feet high. The Town of Rockport and the U. S. Fish and Wildlife Service own the island jointly. The reader will find an abundance of information, along with an

excellent collection of photos, in a 2009 book entitled *Twin Lights of Thacher Island, Cape Ann*, written by Paul St. Germain.

Rockport volunteers can be seen departing the town float early on Wednesday mornings during the summer months in a specially designed boat that was built for landing on the island. I began making these weekly trips as soon as I returned to Rockport. The opportunity to work with good friends and to be in such a natural environment was perfect for me. I wanted to donate something to the island in memory of my mother, father, sister, and brother. A new flagpole was needed near the landing ramp and boathouse, and this seemed a fitting memorial for me to present to the Thacher Island Association. I drafted a letter to the association, which was read publicly at one of their meetings. When it was accepted, the suggestion was made that I be the one to find a location and erect the flagpole.

This became my personal project during the summer of 2006. I spent the first day clearing brush and locating a place where a hole might be dug in the ground at a sufficient depth for the base of the pole. I found an excellent spot just in back of the boathouse, where the flag would be clearly visible from the mainland. On the other hand, most of the brush I had been clearing that day turned out to be poison ivy, and I was wearing Bermuda shorts and had taken my shirt off. The result was a painful, irritating rash all over my stomach and back.

After several weeks, it was time for all hands to join together to erect the pole. Once the pole was erected and secured I constructed a base, using beach stones and concrete. The final touch was a polished black granite plaque with the appropriate names that I cemented to a large stone at the base.

The spirit of community and of volunteers working together with one common task is a great thing to be part of. The calls of gulls and the gentle lapping of waves upon the shore provide a backdrop for one of the most relaxing ways to spend a day that I can imagine. It is a special treat during the early spring to see where the sea gulls have laid their eggs. They are so used to people being on the island that they hardly move when approached within a few feet. A week later the eggs begin to crack and the process of birth begins to take place. Each week the process continues until, at long last, a baby gull appears, barely able to stand. We watch throughout each summer as the babies learn to fly and become independent. It is important to keep in mind, however, that mother gulls will fiercely protect their young. I was nearly attacked on several occasions because I became a little too casual and approached too close.

I look forward to the spring and the long-awaited first trip to the island after a long winter. There is always some apprehension as to what if any damage has taken place during the winter. The volunteers take it all in stride as they disembark from the launch and begin to assess the situation and make plans for the summer months. Thacher Island is a must for anyone who is visiting Rockport during the summer.

THE SCIENCE TEACHER REAPPEARS

A teacher of general science was needed at a high school in a nearby town, so I decided to apply. My lack of an extensive background in any of the specific disciplines of science limited the subject matter I could teach, but the general science curriculum was familiar to me because I had previously taught it at the middle school. Once again I found myself preparing a classroom and organizing materials for the upcoming year, and it felt good. Because six years had passed since I had last taught, I reviewed the material during the summer. I taught three classes of fourteen to twenty-four students. Usually this included one class of students with learning difficulties and often discipline issues. It did not take long to realize that teaching high school freshmen was very different from teaching eighth grade. There was a dress code at the school, which was to be enforced strictly by the teachers. Some of the female teachers enforced the code, while others were reluctant to do so. Most of the male teachers made no effort to enforce the code.

One year a good friend of mine raced in a transatlantic single-handed sailing race from Europe to Boston. Each day we studied his progress, taking into account weather, currents, and any other factors that related to science. I saw this as an excellent method of bringing scientific information to the students. I informed several of my fellow science teachers about my project, but they did not seem interested. I suppose that it was not part of their curriculum, so they saw no reason to deal with it.

Many of the older teachers appeared to have little enthusiasm for teaching. During my three years at this high school I heard several teachers openly counting the days until they could retire. On one occasion during a professional development meeting, I was on my way to my classroom to get something when I walked by an open classroom. I looked into the room and noticed a teacher sitting at his desk. I informed him that all the teachers were supposed to be at the meeting for professional development, to which he replied, "I don't do professional development."

This teaching experience was rewarding for me. The students responded positively to my attempts to work with them most of the time. In general, if I showed a sincere interest in them and supported them, they would join in and contribute to the class in a positive way. An example of this occurred on a Friday afternoon, when I was tired and looking forward to a relaxing dinner with Sally. A student asked me if I was going to attend a night football game under the lights in Gloucester. I said that I would be there and root for the team. A teacher often must do things on his or her own time in order to show the students that what they do when they are out of school is also important.

The old high school was going to be torn down to make way for a parking lot once a new academic wing was constructed on adjacent ground. At the time I was trying to find a way to reach some of my students who were having a difficult time learning the material. I met with the high school principal and proposed a plan to have the students paint my classroom, an old physics lab that had been painted in a drab color and was extremely dirty. She agreed to the plan and gave me the green light to set my students loose with paintbrushes and their creativity. I explained to my students that the project was a voluntary one that would be accomplished after the normal school day, and I was pleased to see that the students who signed on were the ones who were having the difficulty with academics. There were several students, who weren't in my class, who volunteered for the project.

Each wall showed a mural, depicting various scientific areas of study. The front wall became a mural of outer space, and the back wall represented environmental science. I told one of the volunteers from another class that I wanted a scene of mountains with a waterfall. After I showed her where the paint and brushes were, she went right to work. Within a few short days the wall was transformed into a beautiful idyllic scene.

The school principal informed me that there were no overhead projection screens available for the classroom, so I asked several students to solve the problem. They painted a large square on one section of the wall using flat white paint. In order to add some color, they painted the school colors as a border around the edges. The result was so realistic that several teachers asked me where I had obtained the great screen. The school district superintendent took photographs and commented favorably on what a great job the students had done. It was the perfect way to involve those students, who otherwise would have felt left out of the group. It gave them the opportunity to utilize the god-given talents that each of them possessed.

Often a teacher can make a real and lasting difference in a student's life. On the first day of school one year I noticed a handwritten note in my mailbox, written by the mother of a student from the previous year. The note stated that she was extremely appreciative of the efforts I had made to guide her son while he was in my classroom. She said, "Because of what you have done, my son has begun to want to learn once again." These are the things that make teaching rewarding and worthwhile. There is so much more to being a teacher than simply standing at the head of a class and delivering the course materials.

I had just completed my third year of teaching and was looking forward to the upcoming year when I was told that, due to budgetary constraints, twelve teachers would have to be terminated. I had taught three years, not enough to ensure tenure (or permanent status, as it is now called), so I was one of the twelve who had to go. The issue of tenure, referred to today as "last in, first out," or LIFO, is a controversial one. Once a teacher achieves permanent status, he or she may not be terminated, and many tenured teachers exert only the minimal effort required, knowing that their position is secure. There are large numbers of new teachers who do an exceptional job and work long hours, but they will be the first to go if it is necessary to terminate any teachers. The quality of their work means little or nothing in this situation. I am disgusted when I think of some of those among my coworkers who are most likely teaching today. They arrive just before the bell rings at the beginning of the school day and leave just as soon as possible at the end of the day. This system is much in need of change. It is an issue that is in the news almost daily now, and I believe that change will come soon.

ANOTHER CHANGE

After the first year of teaching I was unemployed during the summer, so I walked the waterfront looking for a seasonal position on the water. I found an opening that required a person holding a license to operate a sail auxiliary vessel upon the waters of Sandy Bay. This was a perfect fit for me, given that I held the requisite license and had experience on board the *When and If*. I began operating the boat called *Appledore III* in the spring with a crew of two, taking tourists for short sails upon the waters of Sandy Bay. I enjoyed the chance to sail all summer and to tell stories about Rockport's history. Here I was sailing with tourists, just as I had done on board the *Scylla* as a young boy.

The owner of the boat enjoyed collecting and studying cannons. He enjoyed firing the boat's cannon when entering port and in the vicinity of the beaches in town. One of my deckhands was a talented and well-qualified girl of college age who had an intense affinity for being around boats. I saw an opportunity to give her a chance to handle the boat soon after I began work. As we were entering the harbor, I asked her when she was going to slow the boat down, and she looked at me with a baffled expression on her face. I told her that I wanted to watch how she handled the boat as we approached the dock, but that she should not be concerned. I would be there if she encountered any difficulties. She did a fine job and felt very proud of herself. It reminded me of the similar situation in Puerto Rico when I was given my first opportunity to handle a tug. Each of us needs an opportunity to demonstrate our skills in life.

AN INTERESTING TWIST OF EVENTS

A few years ago I got the chance to sail from Norfolk, Virginia, to Chestertown, Maryland, on board a large sail-training schooner. I reported aboard in the evening and went below to meet the captain and crew. One of the first people I met was the second mate, who greeted me with a warm hello and a hug. It was the girl who had been my deckhand on board the *Appledore III*. She asked me which watch I would be standing, and I told her that I was assigned to the port watch. She informed me that she would be my watch officer. She had passed the exam and earned a license to operate a sail auxiliary vessel. It took a short while to become accustomed to the switch in roles, but it was fun. I enjoyed watching her do the navigation and piloting and just being her shipmate. I enjoyed having the opportunity to sail a large schooner through the night and get my hands on the wheel.

A NAVIGATION TEACHING POSITION COMES OPEN

After wrapping up my shoreside teaching position, I heard about a position as navigation instructor in the Department of Transportation at Maine Maritime Academy. I applied for the position and made it to runner-up status. A few days later, I received a call from the fellow who had interviewed me for the position, saying that they had had a sudden resignation and were not going to do a job search. They offered me the position because they considered me well qualified. After contemplating the fact that I would have to commute back to Rockport every weekend and live in a small room on board the training ship during the week, I turned down the offer. I often wonder if I should have taken the position.

TUGBOATS ONCE AGAIN

A fter being laid off from the teaching position, I decided to relax during the summer and resume the job search in the fall. In September I joined a towing company that operates over one hundred tugs and barges. My first assignment was as mate on board a boat based in Guayanilla, Puerto Rico. I felt comfortable, as I made my way to the boat, given my familiarity with the area from previous assignments. My room was extremely small, hardly larger than a walk-in closet. This tour of duty began a rotation routine of three weeks on the boat and three weeks at home.

My second assignment was as mate on a large seagoing unit or ATB, an acronym for articulated tug barge. When preparing to get underway, the tug maneuvers into a notch in the barge's stern construction. There is a fitting on the tug's bow that includes a slot and a unit containing two large hydraulic rams. The V part of the notch has a vertical steel rail that fits snugly into the bow fitting. The bow rams are then activated, causing them to come into contact with the steel rail. The total length of the unit when measuring from the bow of the barge to the stern of the tug is 526 feet.

My first trip from Port Everglades, Florida, included anchoring in the Mississippi River for several days while preparing for a job offshore assisting a large offshore oil-drilling rig. After a few days, we proceeded to a point sixty miles offshore, where we lay tethered to the rig by means of a wire, which was attached to the bow of the barge. A meter was fitted on the bow at the point of attachment in order to monitor the tension. A smaller tug maintained the tension on the bow wire of the barge by exerting a constant pull on his wire, which was made fast to the towing wire on the stern of the tug. A floating hose was then connected to the barge manifold, through which the slops were pumped into our barge.

There is no cook on board the tugboats of today, so all hands who wish to volunteer put their names on a chalkboard as chef of the day. I have cooked many meals on board over the past few years and most of them have been quite tasty. One day I cooked a beef stew using potatoes, onions, carrots, and spices. This is the way New England beef stew is cooked, and it is one of my favorite meals. On this particular day the engineer entered the galley, smelled the stew, and immediately said, "Where's the f****** rice? I was amazed that someone thought rice should be included in a beef stew. When I expressed my surprise, he replied, "If you live south of I-90, you use rice." Several of the crew did not like casseroles, which could be prepared ahead of time. There were also several complaints that I left the food in the oven and went to my room. The comment was made that I "did not have my heart in my cooking," so I stopped preparing meals. Usually the ones who do the most complaining are the ones who cook the least.

Living on this large ATB is comfortable with each crewmember living in his or her room. There is satellite television in each room, which really helps to pass the time during off watch hours. The amount of pitching and rolling is minimized by the ATB arrangement, as compared to the smaller, more conventional tugs. Currently, I am on duty and the unit is working in the Mississippi River. It is especially interesting work now, in view of the extensive high levels of the river and very strong currents.

CONCLUSION

A long time goal is finally coming to fruition with the publication of this memoir. I am pleased to have had the opportunity to share many of the stories and remembrances of my life and career and to portray the challenges that the mariner encounters while living two parallel lives.

I was fortunate to have known the course that my career would take at a very early age and often wondered how, as a child, I knew that I was to follow the sea. This life voyage has taken me to parts of the world that I will most likely never see again. The breathtaking sunsets and sunrises in tropical waters were spectacular. Those warm nights while I lay on a wooden cot gazing at the constellations with the cooling breezes drifting over me will always be fresh in my memory. The winter gales in the Gulf of Alaska were awesome examples of the power of the sea.

My career has given me an invaluable opportunity to learn of other cultures in far away lands. My travels have brought me into contact with so many interesting people from all walks of life that it is impossible to name them all. There have been unfortunate moments, as mentioned earlier in my narrative, when I witnessed the sadness and poverty that was prevalent during many of my visits to countries, whose people were deprived of the basic necessities of life. It was sometimes painful for me to have to endure the negative and overbearing characteristics of persons, with whom I have worked in close proximity for extended periods of time. I suppose that I would have had similar encounters, regardless of what career path was chosen. It is obvious to me that the environment on board tended to exacerbate the negative aspects.

I learned much about myself during this voyage and continue to learn more each day. My wife, Sally has been a huge help to me by using her experience and expertise regarding how people learn to help me to see how important it was that I chose the sea for a career. Thanks to her comments and advice, I know that it was the correct choice. Many people unhappily follow career paths for their entire working years. I would not have been professionally satisfied if I was limited to the confines of an office building, and working out of a cubicle. It was essential that I be in an environment that involved hands-on skills. The satisfaction of knowing that I am able to pinpoint my location on this huge globe, simply by the use of a few tables and a sextant is so satisfying to me.

Many factors had to have fit into place, in addition to my decision to go to sea and understanding the reasons for doing so. It was essential that I marry a woman who was strong, independent and trusted. I love my wife Sally now as much as I did during that first summer of 1970. She was the woman who was there for my two girls when they needed the love and attention during their early years. She was there to administer to their hurts and concerns. I know that there was much time spent with trips to the doctor's office, piano lessons, gymnastics, violin lessons and so much more. It was hard for her to keep her chin up on many occasions, while I was away at sea. For all of her support and encouragement, I will always be grateful.

I am thankful for having been blessed with two loving and caring daughters, who have come through this voyage showing understanding and support for their dad. There were long separations when they were young, which were difficult for all of us. I have dealt with many feelings of guilt regarding our life style over the years. There were periods of two to three months when they would not see their dad, which was very hard for them. There were times when their friends would wonder why they would see